THE PROVING GROUND

KARL (BUCK) RODGERS

PAGE PUBLISHING, INC.
Conneaut Lake, PA

First originally published by Page Publishing 2020

ISBN 978-1-64298-899-4 (pbk)
ISBN 978-1-64298-901-4 (digital)

Printed in the United States of America

FOREWORD

Flashbacks often took me to a time before money played a major influence in my life, before the innocents faded. "Neighborhood football or Basketball games, mixed with a round of hide-and-go seek just for a quick feel on a young girl you was crushing for," not a care in the world but to have fun and exert energy the best way we knew how.

But there was a particular time around that era that changed my life forever. An ignition switch that created a spark for my desires to be great and looked up to, respected even.

For the most part, I was always a good kid, some might think otherwise but, "To hell with them 'cause I didn't need their approval."

My mother, being the single parent she is, worked hard to provide the so-called American dream we yearned for; but sometimes, it wasn't enough. Periodically, she would drag us—my siblings and I—to the state office building for assistance from the government. "Yeah, I know, social services equaled *food stamps!*" To some, you would have thought having food stamps was a crime or demeaning. A low standard on society's totem pole if you will.

Now, before this new age technology of the digital era, food stamps used to be distributed in different colored paper currency. A rainbow coalition of tattooed construction paper you would use in a school art project, very colorful and identifiable.

Now, as the young man of the house, mom dukes would send me to the corner store for grocery errands. You know the usual items, such as eggs, bread, milk, etc.

The corner store hung on the east side of the city. Mr. Midz was the hangout. The "Beacon for the Dwellers", if that's what you wanted to call it. From big shots to dope boys, to junkies, and so forth, inhabited this slice of heaven. They felt it was in their eyes. It was always some form of hazing and clowning on the block, especially from the older heads, "outta lessons," in society stature; and this particular day, I would be the next victim, not knowing.

Now, as I made the purchase for the groceries, a burst of laughter echoed throughout the entire bodega, maybe even the block. Rants were being made, as if a circus or parade had come to town, but it did; and I happened to be the clown that day, seeing that I paid the clerk with food stamps. A youngin, not knowing what I had did wrong, stood riddled in guilt and humility. Shortly after the noise came to a cease, one of the older fellas walked up on me and said, "Aye, lil nigga, you can't be serious?" he chuckled.

Still standing in a puzzled trance I respond, "What? What I do?"

"You a man before anything in this world, youngin. Earn yourz before they burn yourz!" he returned. While saying this, pulling out a wad of money wrapped in a rubber band bulging thru the straps.

"You see this, youngin? Dis what it's about, dis right here! Cream!" he shouted.

Waving the money in my face as if he was trying to hypnotize me. Not fully aware, still trembling from the ridicule, a light went off inside me. Instantly, all the emotions I was feeling at that moment created a hungry monster. Not the one that went on killing sprees, but the one whose moves became strategic and decisive. Better then the next to do it. A unique path for my own greatness to be the best. I didn't know what was planned for my future, but all I know it was going to involve three key ingredients: *blood, sweat,* and *tears.*

Coming from a poverty family gave you ambition to do the unthinkable; but in the game that was ahead of us, we had to think, or else all would be a lost.

Now since the birth of the hunger spawned inside me, when the older cat flashed his bankroll, so did the dynasty I was ready to build! "The Proving Grounds." Where you prove your worth!

CHAPTER 1

From the Days of Old

Hazard county circa 1981. Around the time, people was sporting crazy fashion trends. From dyed-teased hair to loud non-matching color outfits. Sneakers with fat shoe laces, anywhere from Reebok to Nike etc. Jewelry dripping on such like royalty, that's how you knew who was doing what. Four-fingered rings with their names sprawled across was a common design along with a dookie-rope gold chain, a combination at its finest. And, let's not forget the track suits and Kangol buckets that came in different flavors like a pack of starbursts. Those were and still very trendy to this day. The fashion styles at these times was endless and timeless to the new age.

Lenny, Clintwood, and Laylo was three common by day hard workers; but by night, three the hard way, trying make a dollar by any scams possibly that fell into their laps.

A couple strong arms to smuggling contraband on the back end was just a little mischief they brewed in. Clintwood was a laid-back kind of guy, just down for the cause to put money in his pockets. Laylo and Lenny was the grimy two who fed off each other's negative antics, scheming and scratching to the top of the street chain. Back when Washington park was the *pink buildings,* they housed the first stance of these projects, running it like their headquarters setting up shop. They were one of the four father locally. Laylo had a side gig running back and forth to Augusta and other parts of Georgia, transporting cars and fixing them. He had access to the southern region more frequently than the two others. Lenny was a welder at one of the local warehouse plants in the county, making a small wage. All three met in middle school, a few years back playing parks and recreational sports, eventually, that's how they became friends.

Laylo just recently returned from a trip from down south, telling Lenny he just met a connect on the crack game tip. The crack game was an era that was inevitable to withstand. A new drug for new times and culture flips. This drug fell into the lap of America dramatically and drastically.

"Daddio, what's hattenin?" went Laylo. He could see Clintwood walking up behind Lenny as he spoke.

"Solid, my brother, solid!"

"How 'bout you cat?" answered Laylo.

"I'm good, could complain, but who gives a shit, you dig it!" Lenny answers. "Jus' waitin' fo' dis money to fall from da sky!" He chuckled.

"Diggsville! But check it, I met some black nigga that has his hands on some crack, and he's willing to fuck wit' me as long as I run for 'em," spitted Laylo. "Imma snatch it up on da next go round, whatcha think home skillet?" he asked.

"Shit, dat sounds like heaven to my ears, Daddio. Hell yea?" answered Lenny. "Who's da cat?" he asked.

"Don't kno', some bama-ass nigga!" Laylo answered. "Met 'em at one of da shops I delivered to, him and his woman. And his woman, Lord have mercy, she's finer den frogs hair, I tell you!" he boasted.

"Oh, yea. I dig. I dig!" replied Lenny. He was laughing because he always played the lover boy role like he was Pretty Tony himself. God's gift to women as he would say often.

"Well, make it happen!" spitted Lenny. "I got your back if you need it, ya dig!"

"Cool, Daddio, cool!" ended Laylo.

Time went by as the three made a name for themselves with being the gateway to the new age epidemic of crack spreading thru their city. Lenny kept his word to help Laylo move the crack and keep things afloat. They were doing so good that soon, Lenny knew more about the operation of the *Bama-ass nigga* he would so call him. He found out his name was SC, an acronym rather, guessing that that was the initials to his actual name. Lenny also found out that Augusta was the city the crack was coming out from. How he knew was because he went on a few road trips with Laylo just for a safety precaution. He never met SC face-to-face because he wasn't invited to yet. So when it came down to business, Laylo was the only person doing the exchange. It kind of put an animosity feeling over Lenny, seeing that he, in fact, was one of the ones helping get rid of his product.

He figured he should have a seat at the table, and Laylo told him he would, in due time; but he had to wait because SC said so. Lenny trusted Laylo of course, but the sheer thought of greed always clouded his judgement. But in any event Laylo would have Lenny's back before anything. All he could think about was plotting to get next to SC to see who, and how he moved, to study his movements, and see what he was worth. Find out everything about the cat then rob him blind. Kill him even if he has to, just for the disrespect he was feeling.

More time came about, and as time progressed, so did Lenny's fire for getting to SC. He knew it was a matter of time before he got close to him and make his move, because Laylo told him SC invited him and Clintwood down to a southern hospitality event he was throwing, basically a BBB or triple B big backyard barbecue with flamboyant characters spilling their drinks and stories. Nonetheless, the trio was in the building and that was enough to get started with for Lenny.

Now, by the time the barbecue went down, Lenny finessed SC at his home gathering making him comfortable and trustworthy of Lenny. He welcomed him with open arms just as he did Clintwood. They all laughed and drank like old war buddies or as if they know each other for some time, giggling and chuckling like school girls having a blast. Lenny was enjoying himself of course, physically; but mentally, he still was bound by deception. He still had a plan to execute so he felt. Thru the mist of the entourage and conversations going on, Lenny spots a lady, making eye contact instantly. He gazed for a distance, as did she to where it was noticeable and broke the conversation between the fellas. SC turned and saw who Lenny was staring at, his lady Erica. He didn't take offense, but he made his dominance known by calling her over to them, "Hey, E, get your ass over here!"

Her gaze broke once SC shouted for her to come, now turning into a more of a pouting, sulky mode, not really trying to be noticed that she didn't want to be bothered.

"What Stanley?" she replied as she walked up to the group.

"Bitch, whadda fuck you mean, what Stanley? Get yo ass over, and meet my peoples! You dumb hoe! Don't make me embarrass you in front of all these people!" SC rambled.

The trio stood as they watched SC humiliate her in silence, becoming shocked to his disrespect towards her, especially Lenny. After she introduced herself, she excused herself by going to the back bathroom. Lenny watched as she walked away, not paying attention to what was going on in front of him no more. When the coast was clear, Lenny put on his radar cap and located Erica in the bathroom still. Casually and charismatically, he charmed the pants off her with his witty humor and good looks. So much that he ended up having sex with her that very moment in the bathroom. A spark between the two ignited right then, and there. She knew SC was only worried about his business and not her happiness. She was vulnerable to Lenny and felt she could trust him. SC didn't notice they were gone because he was attending to the rest of his houseguests. He was playing host while Lenny was in his bathroom getting served by his woman.

After, it was all over, and the two disbanded. Lenny felt invincible now. One, because he now met SC for his original plan to carry out; and two, because he just had sex with his lady. A double whammy that made him feel untouchable and more dedicated to his plot. For now, he had the man main squeeze in the palm of his hands. He could now use her knowledge and infiltrate SC to find out where he kept his stash. A win-win situation for him is how he saw it, get some pussy in the meantime and get closer to SC money.

The rest of the party went on as planned, a fun filled event with hot smoking barbecue and liquor that ran like a river. No one was the wiser to the disappearance of Erica and Lenny, so the rest of the night, was coy.

A few months passed as the trio now made the transports together down south back to their city, giving Lenny more access to SC now. He started having a secret affair with Erica behind SC back, being discreet about it when he came down. Also, she would come see him when she would visit her mother who stayed in New Jersey on the pass thru. A reason or excuse to get away to see Lenny from time to time. Laylo knew about the love affair that was going on but didn't care about it because he knew that was Lenny's demeanor, but he didn't know what else Lenny had planned other than fucking the nigga old lady. More so, he didn't care to know, so he kept his mouth shut and continued to keep shit moving as normal.

Over the course of the few month love affair between the two, Lenny swindle and manipulated Erica's mind to help him rob SC. He promised he would come for her and take care of her for the rest of her days. She mentioned that she seen a vault full of money underneath the bed but couldn't tell Lenny how much it was, just it was a lot. That made Lenny more anxious to go thru with his plan. Erica just wanted to be treated like a queen and spend the nigga who was doing it money, but the downside of things was she didn't know the combination code, so they were going to need SC to be present. Might even mean offing him.

Later that night, Lenny sparks up a cigarette and takes a puff while walking up to Laylo who was standing on the balcony of the hotel room they were staying in.

"Daddio, you can say yay or nay but we're gettin da bama tonight!" Lenny went.

A look of amazement comes out of nowhere from Laylo like he heard something he was waiting to hear.

"Really, cat? How you manage to do dis?" replied Laylo.

"Erica!" Lenny said.

"Ooohhh! Should've known you and them bitches, cat!" replied Laylo. "Fuck it no introduction, count me in. I'm tired of da bama anyway!" he added.

Clintwood could over hear the two from the room, and when they turned to him, the answer on his face gave him a way that he was in also.

"Tonight then!" ended Lenny. Now that everybody was on board, Lenny heads to the payphone and calls Erica to tell her the plans.

Ring! Ring! "Hello," Erica answered.

"Baby doll, we gon' do it tonight. Be ready, aight?" went Lenny.

"I don't kno' 'bout it baby. I'm sick, and I don't kno' if it's because I'm scared to or if I'm pregnant. My period ain't come last month!" she spat.

Lenny heard what she said but brushed pass the fact and manipulated her to get her shit in order. Tonight was now or never in Lenny's eyes, and the plan was being executed tonight. He had it all set up to rush SC when Erica unlocked the back door for them. Undetected and unnoticed to float thru SC five-bedroom house. It was one gun amongst the three of them. A .38 special that Lenny always carried for protection. It was around 11:30 p.m. when they invaded SC's home, figuring he would be sleep at that time, at least that's what Erica had told him. Laylo was holding the gun in the caper so that way Lenny would have freedom to do the pushing and mushing around. Clintwood was the getaway driver who was waiting outside. The two crept in silently all the way to SC's master bedroom where he was lying. Erica already had left the house as planned, waiting to hear when the ordeal was over with; but to their surprise, SC wasn't asleep, he was sitting at his desk doing paperwork.

The two bum rushed in grabbing SC, slamming him to the ground holding him at gunpoint.

"Don't move!" they screamed thru the scuffle.

Lenny instantly went to the bed and flipped it over, exposing the safe Erica was talking about.

"What's da combination?" Lenny screamed.

SC didn't say nothing, trying to be stubborn and resentful all in one.

"What da fuck y'all thinking?" he said. No masks on, seeing that it was Lenny and Laylo. Still not giving up the code, Lenny signals Laylo to smack him with the gun. "Crakkk!" SC's head jerked, and blood started squirting out from his face.

"Ahhh, mudddafucka!" SC yelped but still, not saying a word. All that was in his mind was how the fuck they made it in this far to his safe. That's when it hit him, Erica was the inside man. "Damn dis bitch!" he said to himself. "Set me up and wit deez niggas at dat!"

Before you knew it, another smack came across SC's face. *Thonk!* His head swung again, spilling more blood out now.

"Stop stalling, nigga!" screamed Laylo.

They still could see that he wasn't giving up the code, so they put a motivational tool to use by shooting SC in the leg. *Pow!* The bullet rips thru his thigh making him bounce on the ground like a fish flapping out of water. "Ahhh, shit, fuck!" SC blurted.

"Don't make me blow your shit off! Jus' give us da code, and we out!" screamed Lenny.

"Aight, aight. It's 24,14, 32, shit!" he finally answered.

Lenny turned the knobs to the numbers SC said, unlocking the safe latch. When he opens it, his face starts to glow with excitement. He then pulled out the trash bags from out his pocket and started to empty the safe. Laylo still had the gun on SC while he was holding his leg where he was shot at. After filling the bags up with the money, they then proceeded to break out and leave SC alone, no more harmed than he already was; but one thing changed that when he said to the two as they were leaving, "Don't think dis shit over wit. Imma catch you, ahhh!" Still in pain from the leg shot. The two stopped in the doorway and looked at each other like they were forgetting something, which they were, their street morale. They couldn't let this nigga live and come back and get revenge on them, so they knew they had to kill him. Lenny took the gun out of Laylo's hand without hesitation, turned back to SC and pointed the gun at his head. *Bang!* the gun went off again, striking SC in the head with the bullet. His body lay back motionless.

The two broke out like a thief in the night, hopping in the car with Clintwood blazing tracks thru the streets.

CHAPTER 2

The Saga Begins

Some nostalgia was in the air, as Pooh was getting ready for the first day of school. Around the time, Jay-Z had the radio airwaves on lock listening to "Can I live" chanting along with the lyrics, also his hand moving systematically to the beat as he ironed his clothes. Posters of greatness is staring at Pooh while he was getting ready, icons such as Malcolm X, MLK Jr., and Michael Jordan was just to name a few. Midnight, who was Pooh's faithful companion, *his dog* literally, was also watching Pooh as he performed his own private concert in the privacy of his room. Midnight's eyes illuminated the night like he was born with night vision goggles or something. *Creepy sometimes,* Pooh thought, *but cool, nevertheless.*

Now, why was I excited? Pooh thought to himself.

Maybe the fact of going back to school, seeing the fellas and sporting off his new fashion. "I mean, you have to stunt on the first day back, ya kno'!" He chuckled to himself. Or the fact that he was a calculating machine on the low, and he loved to gain more knowledge to his advantage for greater benefits. Either way, a surge of energy was streaming thru his veins. *It's gonna be a good day.*

While thinking so, Pooh's pager went off. It's Graph, Pooh's cousin. How he knew it was Graph hitting him, he could tell by the code Graph was using. Now Graph and Pooh was peas in a pod, where you seen one, nine times out of ten you would see the other.

Maybe dis nigga tryna figure out the route to school dis morning. Lemme hit 'em up!

Ring. Ring.

"Yo, what's really good?" Graph yelled into the phone.

"Yo," Pooh responded in a monotone voice.

They were blood cousins, technically speaking but more like blood brothers in reality.

"What's da move for da morning?" Graph asked before he began choking.

"You already chiefin huh?" Pooh asked.

"Hell yea, what u mean nigga?" laughed Graph, choking even harder now.

"I'm gonna to be higher den a giraffe's ass but still fresh to death. Ya heard, cuz!' Pooh chuckled. "You a fool nigga. I can dig it tho, bro!" Pooh was laughing 'cause he knew Graph was dead serious but also mad at the fact Graph started smoking without him.

"What u rockin? Da buttas wit da Guess jeans, cuz?" asked Pooh.

"Yea, da same pair I grabbed you. bro. Shit, I got dem for a good price," returned Graph.

"Oh, aight, aight! Shit sounds like a plan fam. How you gettin to school tho dis morning? Niggas talkin 'bout walking, meeting up at da overpass," added Pooh.

The phone goes silent for a brief second. *I know dis nigga ain't say walk, did he?* Graph was thinking to himself. Pooh could tell he had caught his cousin off guard by the awkward silence.

"Yo!" screamed Pooh. "Graph, did you hear me?"

Graph snapped back into the conversation. "Fuck it. Yea dats cool. I jus' seen Rizz and Jay at da Laundromat, so I know dey ready to mob. I'll meet you up there by seven thirty. Aight?" went Graph.

"Bet my nig, I'm waiting on Luck then we out," returned Pooh.

"Bet" finishes Graph as they both smoothly hang the phones up.

Pooh was looking in the mirror, going over his last-minute touches. A fresh haircut from Mr. Kelly's barbershop was the norm. A must have before you went back to school.

So after rapping to Graph, Pooh proceeds back to getting ready. His mother, Momma Maggie or Momma Mag for short, had breakfast waiting on the table, a spread fit for a king. A special type of occasion banquet event for her son because she was proud that he was striving for higher learning aspiring to do something with his life and future. Not to be a has been.

A knock came to the front door. It's Luck as he peeks his head thru the door. "Good morning, Momma Mag," went Luck.

"Good morning, baaabbyyy! There's some food in dere on da table, baby, if your hungry." she added.

"Why, thank you, Momma. Don't mind if I do," returned Luck. "Where's ur knucklehead son at? He still ain't ready?" added Luck while helping himself to the delicious breakfast spread before him.

"You kno' dat boy, and his timing chileee," laughed Momma Mag. "Please don't gemme started." She chuckled. They both chimed in, laughing together.

By the last bite that Luck took, Pooh steps out the room. "You always feedin your face, fat boy!" screamed Pooh in a jokingly manner.

"Oh, hush, chump. Is you ready?" returned Luck. "I'm tryna get it like you baller!" Another burst of laughter echoed the house. This time it included Pooh as well. "Let's go, bro. We gon' be late," went Luck.

"Nah, we good we gon' walk today, gotta meet da fellas," Pooh replied.

"You not gonna eat, Pooh?" asked his mother.

"Don't got time, mom, gotta meet Graph at the store. We're walkin to school," responded Pooh.

"Ok, baby, make sure you eat somethin, Alright?" she added.

"Don't worry, mom, I will," responding back while kissing his mother on the forehead.

Pooh turns to Luck, "You ready?"

"Let's roll," replied Luck.

"See you later, Momma Mag," went Luck.

"Bye, boys."

"Bye!" went the boys as they walked out the house.

Luck and Pooh walked up the block towards the store, Mr. Midz. It was on the way towards their fair high school. As they were getting closer to the store, they bump into Rizz and his little but awkwardly big cousin OJ. OJ being the little cousin always played Rizz's shadow, trying to learn the ropes, knowing that his cousin was a go-getter by any means to grease his pockets.

"What's goodie?" went OJ while sparking up the blunt that was hiding in his ear.

"Fellas! Fellas! What's da deal? I see niggas is out dis bish early huh?" laughed Pooh. Rizz shaking his head in agreement. "You already, sleep is for da weak!" he added.

"Yea, school came back early huh?" went OJ.

"Niggas worried 'bout dem books. I'm worried 'bout dis money ya heard!" blurted Rizz.

The group laughs at Rizz for the fact they knew what he meant by saying that.

Pooh responded, "I can dig it, big homie; but don't worry, we got dat thing lined up tonight so we should be good," added Pooh. "An after-party for the after-party if you catch my drift, bro."

Rizz lights up like a christmas tree. "Oh, word!" said Rizz. Rubbing his hands like he's trying to keep them warmed up or spark a fire with his palms. "Shiddd, I hope it's something lucrative, don't wanna have to kick n da door like Biggie!" he added. Again, the group bust out laughing.

"Dis nigga crazy!" laughed Luck.

"We on da way to meet Graph at da overpass," went Pooh.

"Yea, I rapped to 'em earlier. Told em I'll meet him up there after I hit dis lick," returned Rizz.

"Bet, well we out then, fam," finished Pooh.

We could spot Manny and Blake across the street posted in front of the housing units called "Da Greens." A trap spot where Luck and his fellas would hang out at.

These two were part of Luck's affiliation.

"What's da deal?" yelled Blake.

"You big headed fucker you!" Luck shouted back. More chuckles erupted between the two groups now.

15

"Fuck you!" screamed Blake. Slightly embarrassed by Luck's sly comeback joke for even Manny was laughing at him now.

"What's goodie, fellas?" went Manny as the fellas was approaching them.

They dapped each other with a few handshakes and fist bumps. "Ain't shit. New day, new year, and dat means new money Pooh.

"Amen to dat ish," went Blake.

Manny was more of the brains for Luck while Blake was no doubt the muscle, but either way, a dynamic trifecta.

"Well, we still gotta meet niggas up da street so we out!" went Pooh.

As we approached the overpass which was located next to the train station. Da overpass was a bridge that separated our fair city into two sides. You have the west side, and then you have the east-side. Southside and Northside was mainly out of towners or out of staters, but nevertheless, a part of our quaint city of Hazard. The six of us began to walk, coming up on the Aberdeen Village housing development that sat right in front of the train station and da overpass. Now, them (AVB) *Aberdeen village boys* was a group of different skilled talents. You had two sets of twins that were the ball players climbing the stat sheets in the county. Then you also had a few of the rest of the *AV boys* that were hustling by any means to make a dollar for a come-up. A bunch of cool cats, in all actuality more like an extended family of the streets. I mean, at them times it felt like everyone was family or related somehow one way of or the other.

We have seen them standing alongside of the road that led us to da overpass. It looked like they were waiting for the school bus to come to scoop them up.

"Okay, I see niggas lookin' fresh, shiddd!" blasted Roach. One of the AV boys head money making niggas, also standing next to him his comrade Blue, who was also known to get a dollar.

"Tryna live broskie, tryna live," replied Luck. "We see who's really gettin' it!" he added, laughing and bragging at the same time.

"Y'all waiting on da bus? Cuz we 'bout to walk. Graph's around da corner waitin fo us," interrupted Pooh.

"Bet we'll mob. We got something to spark up anyways, let's do it," returned Roach. Blue nodded his head in agreement.

We took a couple more steps, and through the blind side of things, here comes the *WP Mafia boys*.

Now you didn't have to lay eyes on them to spot them coming 'cause really you heard them coming. Loud as hell, obnoxiously ranting and raving like a choo choo train, a walking mosh pit to be exact. Rowdy bunch of niggas who resided in the projects known as *Washington park* thus giving the acronym of WP. The mafia come from the trending times of famous gangster movies. Guess it was added for the bone-chilling thrill to strike fear in whoever opposed them.

Now, leading the pack was Graph of course. Behind him following was his boys Vito and Trav, two blood cousins who were day and night when it came to their personalities. Trav was an ill-tempered type of dude, a down for whatever type of nigga; and Vito was more of a laidback type of cat. I mean, don't take Vito's kindness for weakness. If you crossed him, he was down for the get back no doubt. Graph also had a couple of young boys with him who was always trying to prove their loyalty at any moment or cost just to impress him. Graph kept them around for minor things, nothing major.

Church was in session. The conglomerate was in full effect for the first day back to school. Of all things, about twenty to thirty deep give or take. Felt like a mini militia, an untouchable but empowered force by invincibility. *A force not to be wrecking with.*

"Ayeee, what's da deal, my niggas!" screamed Graph while exhaling the weed smoke thru his jaws.

"Pass dat!" replied Pooh. "Lemme hit somethin. Matter fact I'm 'bout to twist up," he added.

The groups huddled around like a block party was going on. Clouds of smoke started appearing over the heads of the circled pack. Look like a comic strip, but no words were written.

"Don't forget we got dat thing lined up tonight," went Graph. Reminding Pooh and Luck for tonight's affairs that was planned. Everyone else was thinking Graph was referring to the back to school parties that was lined up later that evening.

"Oh, no doubt. We on it!" returned Pooh, and Luck shaking his head in agreement taking a big inhale off the blunt he was smoking.

"Bet, well niggas betta start movin' before we late!" finished Graph.

We were mob deep now walking to school, where we knew it was strength in numbers. We could outnumber you, a ten to one ratio, at anytime. Don't be dumb to this, I mean if one hyena fights then the rest is bound to get in. It was a GP, general principal code, that the streets went by, especially from block to block around our city. You couldn't walk in nobody else's kitchen and go in there refrigerator without permission and not suffer the repercussions or consequences. That's anywhere on this ball we call Earth. We weren't a gang, we were an extended family. A round table of knights around the city, but no one could hold the Excalibur blade. Everyone was eager to, but who, was the better question to ask. A fairytale that soon would come to reality, from a frog to a prince. Everybody have the taste for clout and fame at some point in their lives. Just to be noticed and recognized was a great feat for some. It would always be competition, one way or the other, whether it's an opposing side or animosity that builds within the family walls. Inevitable for it was shared in the Bible, "brother killing brother to a friend's betrayal". So what was the difference in life to us, nothing but to stack and pray. Most of the parents tried keeping their kids in church, that's how some of the fellas met around the way. Using Sunday school as a front for a hang out.

Mr. Booker was the bus driver who came to pick the kids up around the town. Only reason the kids really went was one, their parents forced them to, and two was, Mr. Booker would take the kids to McDonald's for breakfast after sermon. Days for fun and not really paying religion too much mind because they felt it was a bore. No disrespect to the Bible or God, it was just that their attention span wasn't long enough for the theatrics of praising the Lord. Give glory of course, but to give time was kind of hard to, especially as a kid around their temptation years. The chain soon eventually broke as some strayed to the dark side to find whatever it was they were looking for. Some would return changed; and others would be lost for the rest of their days not finding themselves, and whatever their journey was for. A sad cycle, but nevertheless, a road that was often traveled upon coming from our era and city. A ritual or Rights of passage to all. Whether blue, white, or black collar, this was a time to come. The next generation was bound to step up, to do it better than the ones before them and they were certain to do so.

CHAPTER 3

Home of the Birds

School bell rings. Mrs. Kennedy's class.

And it just so happens that this school year, the trio ended up in the same class: Pooh, Luck and Graph. How ironic.

Now Mrs. Kennedy was there English teacher, a short petite but curvy-shaped woman with a pair of glasses that gave her the naughty teacher look. Ready to punish us with rulers and detention.

Shidd, she could punish us anytime, we thought. I mean with an apple for an ass who wouldn't want to be her teacher's pet. Seriously!

The class was obnoxiously loud with desks clomping and chairs screeching, not to mention the banter of the classmates talking, overwhelmed with reacquainting with old friends not settling down.

"Settle down, class, Settle down!" went Mrs. Kennedy.

Getting the attention of the classroom.

Now, as she turns to the chalkboard to start the morning assignment drills exposing sight of what the good Lord blessed her with, briefly distracted by our teenage hormones, we snap back to reality.

Graph wanted to pep talk with us to go over tonight's details, so he waited for the perfect time for when Mrs. Kennedy wasn't paying attention and started to speak.

"Now remember tonight we meet dis new plug. We need everything to go right, ya dig?" went Graph.

"No doubt, you kno' da nigga. What's da nigga name?" replied Pooh in a concerned manner.

"Da nigga name is Southern Comfort, some bullshit like dat, but it don't matter. I met 'em thru Luke before he got sent up da road. He vouched he's good peoples," Graph returned.

Luck gives a little chuckle, amused by the plugs name. "Chill out!" blurted Graph.

"No time for games, bro," he added.

"No doubt, bro. I'm wit u!" cried Luck.

"Now, if everything goes smoothly tonight, we should be looking good by the morning," finished Graph.

"Bet!" went Pooh and Luck at the same time.

"Be on standby. I'll keep y'all posted, Aight?" Graph added.

"Cool!" went everybody.

School bell rings to let the class out for the lunch.

"Yo, you got an extra punch on your lunch ticket?" Graph asked Luck while standing in the lunch line.

"Nah, my nigga. Dis is for me," Luck returned laughing.

"Ah you dickhead!" responded Graph. As he was approaching the cashier, he pulls out his money. A knot wit a few hundreds wrapped around in a roll. He gets the total from the lunch lady, $8.14. The smallest bill he had was a $100 bill.

He proceeded to hand the lady the bill when she replied, "Honey I don't have change for that." Graph gave a horror look like he was denied his rights for food, but before he could speak out, Pooh slides the lunch lady a $10 bill.

"Don't worry, cuz. I got you!" went Pooh.

"Good look, bro!" replied Graph.

"You stuntin so hard you can't even eat." Laughed Pooh. Graph shakes his head, not in disappointment but in accordance that Pooh was right. He had money and couldn't even pay for the meal because he had no smaller bills. "Yea, you doing too much, bro." again goes Pooh.

After lunch, school breezed by. All you could remember was the hallways decorated with blue and gold settings and the posters for the upcoming Homecoming event.

Fast little niggas we were! Graph always had some shit cooking up. Figuratively! The deal was to meet the plug and make the

arrangements later after the *back to school party's*, and put the shipment in motion. Graph told the fellas we were to meet at the Red
Roof Inn, room number 221. Ask for "Southern Comfort." A mild
laugh played inside of us. Seemingly, everything was in place, ready
to have fun and get prepped for the beacon. The only question was
which party to hit tonight. I mean you had a few spots that was
popping, such as the Legion, you also had the DYA that sat on the
Armed force base, And then, there was Vibrations. Now, us being
minors by nature, we technically couldn't get into Vibrations or the
Legion due to alcohol restrictions, but Graph had his ways to work
magic. He had connections to get in either one of the clubs. The
point of the matter was which one though. Pooh figured that Luck
and his squad was going to DYA since his mother was a soldier active
duty on the base. *Figure I'll catch up wit 'em later*, Pooh thought to
himself.

Graph breaks Pooh's train of thought. "Yo, cuz, flip a coin.
Heads we go to da Legion or tails, we go to Vibrations. Pooh took
a coin out his pocket and proceeded to flip it. It lands ringing and
clinging on tails.

"Vibrations it is!" screamed Graph. Either way both clubs was
going to be lit no matter the options.

"Bet!" announced Pooh.

"Fresh to death like a million bucks!" was the theme when we
stepped out. All eyes on us was the objective, but when our alter ego
side had to come out, we were more on the L.O.X.'s Wild Out type
of tip. A bull who spots a red cloak.

Soon as you stepped in the building, you could smell the aroma,
a mixture between fried food and weed smoke.

"Make way fo' some real niggas!" screamed Pooh as Graph and
him make their way thru the crowd. Doing a step just to feel the
rhythm of the music. "My God!" They had DJ Coogi's best creations
blasting out the speakers. Meanwhile, the host on the microphone
was hyping the crowd up even louder. When I mean one of three best
DJs hands down that blessed the city with his craft and artwork. I'd
still bet money. He could rock the roof of the spot!

Females in all shapes and sizes, from light to dark plagued the scene. Just saying, it wasn't no discriminating when it came to getting pussy, but the fellas could spot that Malisha and Tawana was in the building. These two chicks were the boy's counterparts, a female version of Pooh and Graph that stuck beside them since junior high school. Some of the baddest chicks to grace our school hallways.

"What's up, my future Baby momma?" went Pooh as he approached Tawana.

"Boy, you silly." Laughed Tawana, playing a coy but hard to get type of roll, loving the fact that Pooh would play cat and mouse with her.

Graph approach was more stern; and smoothly, how he slid his arm around the back of Malisha's neck, guiding her off so they could be alone. Well, that's another story for later.

Now, as the night lingers on, Pooh pages Luck, 11:45. We were to meet the plug at 2:00 a.m. at the Red Roof Inn. Pooh didn't pay no attention to the nonresponse from Luck, figuring it was still early in the night.

The party was over at one. Graph taps Pooh on the shoulder leaning over, showing him he just got the page from Southern Comfort, indicating everything was a go for the night.

"Bet I'm jus' waitin' fo' Luck to hit me back," went Pooh.

"Aight, well, we in motio,." added Graph.

Time winded down close to closing time.

"Last call!" went the bartender.

Pooh realizing it was 'bout that time to leave, he takes a look at his pager. *Damn, Luck never responded*, he thought to himself, getting a little worried now. *Maybe dat nigga fell in some yams. Psst, dis nigga here.* Nevertheless, moves had to be made, and Pooh knew this.

As the duo was leaving out the club they bump into Rizz and his underling Jay.

"What's good, familia?" went Graph in a drunk tempered tone.

"Ain't shit you tell me, fam," returned Rizz.

Jay was behind Rizz, using him as a shield so no one could see him rolling up a blunt. The police had a knack for surprise pop-ups, and everyone had to play cautious.

"'Bout to go buss dat move so be waitn' fo' me on da strip," blasts Graph.

"You sure you don't need me to go with you? You kno" I got your back, my nig," returned Rizz. Showing a little concern in his voice for Graph's safety.

"Nah, we good, jus' be waitin' fo' my signal," replied Graph.

"Shit gets funky. I kno" where you at," he added.

"Cool, broskie. Jus' making sho you good," finished Rizz.

It was a good thing to have the two on their sides because Rizz and Jay were ruthless. Meaning, they would get dirty for a dollar and didn't care who gave a fuck! Better to have them then to be against them. At least that's what Graph thought. In fact, we were all riders for each other. You have to protect the home front. It's a must!

Parking lot flickered with different strobes of lights like a disco dancefloor for the outside. As everybody was dispersing in the directions of their vehicles. Some drove their own vehicles, others rented cars from their favorite neighboring junkies or got chauffeured around by them, depending on the trust or the grade of quality your cocaine was. The *scragglers* hopped in or hopped a cab.

All Pooh could think about was the task at hand, so they sent their girls home by a cab. Graph had happened to rent a fiend named Gerald car for the planned affairs that evening. A Ford Taurus I believe really, not paying attention to detail just ready for the meeting. Nothing major, a simple family-oriented type of transportation to keep under the radar from the law enforcements.

Graph passes Pooh a lit blunt while exhaling the smoke from his mouth he said, "Keep yo' eyes peeled and stay sharp. Don't no what dis nigga could be about, ya dig. Say no mo, broskie. I got u,"

Pooh said before taking a pull off the blunt. The only thing that was clouding Pooh's mind was how did Graph get next to this nigga Southern Comfort. He knows Graph can pull strings somehow but the magnitude of the work was baffling. "*Three bricks was a lot, especially off of consignment. I don't kno', but all I kno' is I got my cuzzin's back*," Pooh was thinking to himself.

The car was approaching closer to their destination on the far west side of the city. The hotel sat right along the highway exit leading to Interstate 95. When Graph pulls into the parking lot of the hotel, he circles the building being cautious because it was known that law enforcement officials would post up in this part of the region.

Soon as Graph sees that the coast was clear, he parks the car, 1:52 a.m. right on time they both thought. That's when Graph mentions to Pooh about Luck. "Where's dat nigga Luck at? Did he hit u back yet?"

Pooh snatches his pager off the hip and takes a look. "Nope, nuttin yet, bro. Don't kno" but hope dat nigga is aight," replies Pooh.

"Fuck it! We work to take care of," finishes Graph. The two finds the room number 221. Graph knocks on the door and waits for the outcome.

Other side of the city, the east side, cars started pulling up on the block. Unflooding the strip with unsavory characters, *Night Scratchers*, if you will. Anywhere from the prostitutes to wannabe pimps to stick up kids. "A concoction of out of lesson ingredients, but nevertheless an economic conerstone.

Rizz and Jay, who normally started out as hustlers originally, soon dabbled in the armed robbery division on the side for an extra come up. Always thirsting for a dollar, these two were posted on the block, waiting on Graph's call.

Rizz tells Jay to spark up the blunt he had rolled on the way to the strip, while he twisted the cap off the Hennesy bottle. Taking a swig, the warm cognac liven Rizz's body with a jolt. Rizz wipes his mouth after he swallows the liquor and said openly, "Where da fuck is da money outchea! Shidd somebody got da deep pockets around here!" he added.

Jay was looking at the blunt like he was studying for an exam, and without making eye contact with Rizz, he responded, "I don't kno', big bro, shit looks dead outchea, but I got word on some niggas moving weight out north. Heard big weight some key playas."

"Word!" blasts Rizz. "And we jus' got dat new hardware in from your peoples. Yea, we need test dat out!" Rizz finishes.

"Cool, Imma look into it some mo', and I'll keep you updated, aight?" added Jay.

"Bet you do dat," went Rizz.

Rizz exhaled the thick smoke in relief. *It was always about the money*, Rizz thought. *Always!*

A junkie by the named Marlene pulls up on the block with one of her tricks in the car with her. Trying to stunt like she was a glorified diva, getting out the car talking her usual bullshit.

"Who got da good shit, and I don't want no small shit!" she screamed.

Meanwhile Klay was out flashing his new Kawasaki ninja motorcycle, doing stunts and tricks up and down the block showing off for the late night audience. Screeching his bike all the way to the max. Now, one of the young pups out on the block must have served Marlene 'cause she was dancing and whaling so much that she wasn't paying attention backing out the parking lot, where she almost side swiped Klay off his bike, sending him of course into the vacant lot that was directly across the street from the bodega. Sending Klay tumbling, you couldn't see where Klay had landed; but you could see where the dust and dirt kicked up at from him crashing.

"Oh, shit, you seen dat?" screamed Niko. "Dat bitch is buggin!" he added.

Everyone rushed to Klay's aide to make sure he was okay. By the time they reached him, he was already standing on his feet staring at his bike in disbelief.

"I jus' bought dis bike today. Psst!" Klay screamed out loud.

Parade noises of "you stupid or you dumb bitch!" echoed the corridor of the narrow strip. Some even attempted to chase down the car Marlene was driving. Crazy right? What you expect for a night on the block surrounded by the vultures and scavengers. The longer the night lingered, the more crazy shit went on. Down the street was where the prostitutes would catch tricks off the highway Rt. 40. A passage thru way for truck drivers and so forth. Each block had its own specifics, known by classification. Anywhere from gambling spots to after hour bootlegging. Casino B would make a killing-off the gambling racket, always conspiring a way to start either a card or dice game. I mean, he didn't get the name Casino B for nothing. Always about a hustle and a dollar, crafty with his moves like a ninja.

Another one of Luck's comrades who plagued the eighty-east corridor where the fellas hung out at. You would normally catch him with his cousin Nigel on sideline heists making a little come up of a stable of bitches also. These two thought they were the Hugh Hefner's of the game, roping up chicks for their pleasures and disposal. "Molding and using but never abusing" was the motto when it came to them finessing their game to these bitches. Doing it for the sport or thrill but never for the love, I mean, niggas was too young to know what love was. Pussy, money, and clothes was the only love niggas felt and that was literally the feeling in their hands and the feelings on their bodies. Mentally, not knowing but physically portraying a false hope or misconception of the term. The old heads always said, "We didn't know what we were talking about" or "We were too fast for our own good."

"Shut up and listen sometimes!" they would say. Or "Why you think you kno' errythin?"

Now in my opinion, I think the old heads was trying to shape you rather than shame you, at least some empathized. Who wanted to see the revolving door of the oppressed and poverty to continue? A simple term of endearment could go a long way, a mother would say. So it was up to that person to apply the knowledge of what was explained, at least to some degree. Some would get the answer and then again, others wouldn't; but God gave you the test, and he was the final person to grade you when it was over with. Life! That is.

CHAPTER 4

Meet and Greet

The door opens slowly, as if it was a slow motion replay from a sports clip. A slim, dark-kinned dude with a bald head answered the door. Graph and Pooh greet the mysterious guy with a "Whaddup!" The mysterious guy didn't respond but gave the fellas a mere grin, exposing what appeared to be a row of gold teeth. Somewhat giving off a strange vibe. *Okay*, we thought as we walked pass him.

"Let's jus' handle dis business then we out," Pooh said to himself. The boys stop in the living room area of the room. Observing the room, being cautious they could only see the mysterious guy in the room. So before the fellas got down to business, assuming that the mysterious guy was the plug a.k.a. Southern Comfort, who they had came to meet, a toilet flushes! A sense of confusion came between the two face, looking at each other puzzled.

We're not alone! they both thought, not noticing that the bathroom door was closed shut. Shortly after they heard the running water turn off, the door opens. The light from the bathroom shined a silhouette of a shadow along the wall like a grand entrance was about to happen. Actually, it was a grand entrance, seeing that the short, stubbled grey-haired man who stepped out the bathroom, wiping his hands with a towel, was indeed Southern Comfort.

"Finally!" we screamed on the inside.

The elderly gentleman, who was dressed in a blazer with the matching slacks to go with his ensemble. A crease so sharp in his pants, it could cut thru a stick of butter. Very old fashion type. Wing tip shoes that looked like they were ready to cut a rug. The elderly gentleman gestures for Pooh and Graph to sit at the table where it appeared to be prepared for a meeting. It was a castle-style type bottle sitting in the middle of shot glasses. Inside the bottle was a brown type of fluid, a cognac perhaps, at least that's what the two thought. The boys take a seat, and before Southern Comfort sits down, he pulls out a cigar, clips it then lights it.

"Welcome, welcome, finally a pleasure to meet you," went Southern Comfort as he's exhaling the smoke from his cigar, hiding behind a sheet of clouds. "Heard good things about you," he added.

"I hope there're good things," laughs Graph, trying to soften up the mood.

Southern Comfort chuckles in a manner like Graph's response was amusing.

"Trust young man, I wouldn't waste my time nor my energy if it wasn't beneficial. One thing, I don't play with my money, you understand?" blurted Southern Comfort.

"We can respect dat, Sir," replied Graph.

"Well then, enough wit da formalities and small talk. Let's get down to bizness," returned Southern Comfort. "A brick is normally going for ten, but on consignment, it's thirteen. That includes travel fees, but if you come grab it, then you can get it at the wholesale price for the ten. Y'all would have to make the arrangements and give me a notice before hand," he added.

Graph and Pooh takes a look at each other for a split second. Telepathically agreeing with each other on the decision to take the work. "We can handle dat, bro," went Graph.

"You sure, cuz?" whispered Pooh.

"Hell yea. Wit da quality alone, it'll sell itself, bro," Graph replied.

"Nigga, I'm wit you either way," finished Pooh.

"Solid!" went Graph. They turn back to Southern Comfort. "We'll take it sir," Graph said.

"Fantastic! But jus' so there's no mix up, I expect my money back in two weeks, dats more than enough time to get rid of dat candy," blasts Southern Comfort. "I have eyes everywhere, young fella, so don't think for a sec I won't kno" what's goin' on," he added.

"No problem sir, not a problem at all," chimed in Pooh.

"Well, good then, glad to hear it. Let's celebrate!" went Southern Comfort.

Southern Comfort signals his associate who the boys forgot was in the room with them, to get the duffle bag that was hiding behind the couch. The mysterious guy goes for the bag while Southern Comfort popped the clasp of the bottle that was sitting on the table. He poured shots for the three of them.

"Salute!" screamed Southern Comfort as he raised his glass to make a toast with his two new young associates.

"Cheeerss!" went Graph and Pooh, clicking all the glasses together making a wind chime noise. They down the shots with ease. By the time, they sat the glasses back down on the table. The mysterious guy hands off the duffle bag to Graph. Graph unzips the bag and takes a peek inside. Three individual wrapped packages containing a thousand grams apiece. Some clothes were thrown in there also, guess to make it look like luggage. Pooh leans over and takes a look. "Hell yea, Bro!" screamed Graph. Zipping the bag back up after his inspection.

"You fellas have a nice evening and be safe, but remember, in two weeks have my money," went Southern Comfort.

Saying this while holding up two fingers like the peace sign but indicating he meant the number two and not peace.

As the two was walking out the door, Graph responded back, "No doubt, Boss Hogg," closing the door behind them.

Before the two got into the car, they stopped by the payphones. Pooh needed to page Zue to have the spot set up for him when he got there, and Graph needed to hit Rizz because he had him waiting on the strip for him. Pooh came to realize that Luck still never hit him back from earlier.

I hope dis nigga not bagged and got drunk and fell into some pussy somewhere, thought Pooh while paging Zue's line. "Yo, I need you to drop me off at Zue's spot bro. Let's go sort dis shit out and get it poppin!" went Pooh.

"Bet dat nigga waitin. We out," replied Graph, heading towards the car ready to skate to the other side of the city. Zue was waiting for Pooh, and Rizz was waiting for Graph.

Zue was a mastermind genius a long side with Pooh, his right-hand man, a calculating chef when it came to cooking up coke. "Cheffin da sauce" is what we called it. I mean, if it could get cooked then Zue was the right person for the job. Graph busted a left onto Roger's ave, right down the street from where Zue was located at. Soon they pull up in front of Zue's spot. They could spot the scavengers hanging around the block. They looked like zombies really. The car comes to a halt and stops.

The two hop out, releasing what clouds that was left over in the car from smoking. They walk towards the front door heading up to Zue's walkway.

Pooh, for some reason kept visualizing and thinking about Southern Comfort's associate, the mysterious guy. *Why was that tho?* Pooh thought to himself. *Maybe the fact he didn't speak or announce his presence but who knows, just odd I think. Oh well,* Pooh pondered, knocking on the door with in a rhythmic pattern.

"Yo, son, you always comin up short! What da fuck is you doin out dere?" yelled Zue. You could hear him from the other side of the door yelling at someone. We could hear him as we approached his door. He was just that upset and loud that his voice traveled outside. Pooh knocks again getting the attention of Zue. Zue's voice began to get louder as he came closer to answer the door for the fellas. "Dumbass!" he screamed as he's answering the door.

"Whaddup, my nigga, you good?" greeted Pooh as they stepped in Zue's place.

"Yea, man, jus' dealin wit dis dumbass in here!" replied Zue, saying all this while leading the two into the dining room area, where they could spot who Zue was screaming at. One of his young boy workers who was fucking up on the packages Zue was giving him.

"Fix your fucking face before I fuck you up, nigga!" blasts Zue. Scolding the young boy even more now, now that there was an audience.

The young boy head hangs a little bit lower. He responds in a low whimpering voice, "Big bro, you kno" I'm good fo' it. I got u."

"Hard workers are harder to find nowadays," added Graph, Laughing at the situation trying to antagonize Zue.

You could see the embarrassment drape the face.

"Chill. Look, lil nigga, dis is your last mufuckin time. You hear! You don't have my money. You won't have your life, ya dig," blasts Zue. "Here take dis and make sure you get at me," he added.

Zue tosses a sandwich baggie that had tan clusters in it on the table towards where the younging was sitting at.

"I appreciate it big homie!" went the young boy.

"Yea, yea, nigga, whateva'. You jus' betta have my money. Now get da fuck outta here!" finishes Zue.

Everyone watched as the young boy took the walk of shame out the front door. Us, standing in amazement watching Zue scold the young boy like a father to a son was priceless. Now that's what was missing, no discipline in the game. Rule with an iron fist.

Still bothered by the younging actions, Graph intrudes Zue's emotions.

"Fuck it. We got work to do, nigga," Graph sad. "I need you to put the spin machine on deez!" he added, lying down the duffle bag on the dining room table. Zue unzipped the bag and took a peek.

"Ooowwweee!" he screamed, getting excited like he just got the gift he wanted on Christmas day. "Dats what da fuck I'm talkin' 'bout right dere! Dem white bitches lookin' mighty fine!" boasted Zue.

"Dats dat grade A, fam, so make it do what it do," returned Graph.

Zue starts clapping his hands like he called a play out of a huddle.

Beautiful, jus' simply beautiful! Zue was thinking to himself.

Pooh could see the excitement in Zue's face. "Told you, nigga," went Pooh.

"Yea, you did, bro!" returned Zue.

"We owe da connect thirty-nine thousand, and we gotta have dat to him in two weeks. So we gonna leave one plain for da skiers, and da otha two, we gonna double dat for da profit. The first one we dump goes to payin da connect off, and da rest we eat off of, Aight?" announces Graph. "Which reminds me, cuz' you still haven't rapped to Luck?" he added.

"Nah still no word," answered Pooh.

"Fuck it. Swing by dere tomorrow and see if he's aight. Fat ass prolly in dere sleep," blasted Graph.

"I gotta go holla at Rizz. He's waitin fo me," he added.

"Aight, bro, say no mo. I got u!" Pooh returned.

Graph pulls the keys out his pocket and turns towards the front door.

"You gonna be straight?" Graph asked Pooh before walking out the door.

"Yea, bro. I'm gravy, you be safe. I'll check you out later and put dis up in da spot when it's done," answered Pooh.

"Bet my nig! Holla!" screamed Graph as he walks out the door.

Zue already had his chemistry set laid out, displaying all his unique utensils. A triple beam, a sifter, and a couple of measuring cups was just a few items to name. Pooh sparked up a blunt while Zue began to get ready for his class project. Dancing and grooving getting into the mood for "Cheffin da sauce."

Pooh exhales the smoke and said, "Yo, cuz, what was dat all about wit da young fella?"

"These nigs are something else, bruh! You jus' never kno'," Zue said.

"That's why they are workers and not owners," responded Pooh looking at the door, in bewilderment, still in an amazement of what had happened.

Zue busts out laughing, saying, "True indeed! They definitely reinforced dat fact! They have to feel like they are gettin over to be satisfied, but in all actuality, they can be useless at times." Zue starts choking on the loud, his eyes filled up with water, and instantly became red.

"Right!" Pooh said as he reaches for the blunt Zue was choking from. Zue extends his hands giving it up with no hesitation 'cause he was still coughing.

"So let their minds stay dat way. They will always be worker bees instead of being bosses, Ya dig," said Pooh while leaning his head back exhaling the weed smoke from his jaws. "No doubt, bruh," Zue said, finally catching his breath.

The aroma from the smoke circulated the room. The blunt was about a clip size by the time Zue began his culinary course.

First, he busts open the tapped package, separating and scaling each brick by ounces. Each brick contain thirty-six ounces apiece totaling up to a hundred and eight ounces between the three bricks. One of the bricks wasn't going to be cooked but distributed the way it was so that was thirty-six the normal way. The other two bricks or seventy-two ounces was going to be doubled into a hundred and forty-for ounces of crack cocaine. A form of a drug that you could stretch your product and money of. The coke was pure enough just to do so.

Pooh got dizzy just from looking at all the coke on the table. "Geez, Louise!" he said to himself. "All dis work, we 'bouta take over da city wit dis here."

It was a method and a strategy to Zue's skills. Every measurement was precise and accurate to a degree. He was very meticulous when it came to this talent. Having good product gives you a good name and bigger clientele in the streets, but it also could be a curse, reason being, it could draw the wrong attention.

Zue turns the stove on. The flames roar. The water hit the pot. The pot hit the stove. The knee bone connected to the thigh bone, it felt like to Pooh as he watched.

"Yo, I'm finna break out and stash dat snow, bro!" Pooh screamed to Zue as he's bagging up the first brick.

"Bet," mumbled Zue for he was hiding behind a doctor's mask trying not to inhale the fumes from the cocaine avoiding a buzz.

"Peace!" Pooh screamed as he walked out the door.

Feeling satisfaction that everything was starting smoothly, he took a sigh of relief. *Finally, we made it!* he thought. *We sittin' at da big boy's table!*

The feeling overwhelmed his body. Now, he didn't have to ask nobody for nothing. Pooh was his own boss, and it felt great he didn't have to answer to nobody as long as the count was good each time for the re-up then everything was official. In fact, he gloated more once the thought had crossed his mind that niggas had to answer to him for the work. He was in control of the west side pipeline slowly creeping up for the complete takeover. Unknowns was always up and coming, thinking they were doing big numbers, but in all really, just a waste of space and time. Now a few things could occur when it came to this which was. One, you can sweetin' up the deal for them, make them cop from you for a cheaper price; or two, you could force them out, straight flood, and drown them out to a point where they can't breath or eat. And the final option was to have them exterminated if they became a thorn in the operation's side. Some people can't be compromising nor negotiable when it comes to making money. Really, nobody wants a boss telling them what to do; but when you in a position to where the next man hand was feeding you, you had no choice but to bow down until your time came or come. So until then, you played your part as the gears that turned the wheels of the street game.

Pooh felt he was top gear in the wheel on the west side because nobody really pushing heavy on that side. All the traffic really swung thru the east side between WP and *Da Greens,* so it was a perfect spot for a new direction of the money flow. Pooh figured he'd be able to corner the *scragglers* that was coming off the highway who stayed in the motels that surrounded the freeway. Motel money was always good. Getting the tourist's money made you feel like you were the attraction, and if you gave them a night to remember, then you would have sear a landmark in their drug taking memoirs. Poetic on one end, but economic on the other; and that was the point, to get to the money and make your stamp known.

You would want to put your family under the umbrella so they don't get soaked, but it comes a time where you won't be able to keep them dry forever. The baby bird has to leave the nest, and you have to let them do fend for themselves.

His main objective was to own his own technology business since the new millennium was approaching, and the wave of technology was switching to a digital format. Pooh knew it wasn't a life-long career in the drug game so he had other plans; but right now, to get him to the next plateau was stacking this money up and moving this coke.

CHAPTER 5

The price of Luck

Light bulbs flicker while a cold chill sweeps the concrete encased room. In front of the room was a glass shield. From the outside looking in, the room looked like a lab-rat experiment cage. Hard wooden benches wrapped around the room in an L shape along the wall. In the corner sat a sink/toilet mixture embedded in the wall.

Luck had his face pressed against the glass door, staring into a daze. "Fuck!" he screamed to himself now realizing the feeling had sunk in that he was locked up.

"Now why da fuck I ride wit dis nigga, knowin he was hot," said Luck. "Dumbass!" he added.

Fortunately, Luck was still a minor and would be released to his parent/guardian. Plus, he wasn't being charged with anything because the person he was with had took full blame to the charges that was being issued. The police just could detain Luck because it was after hours until an adult could come pick him up. Luck was pissed even more now that his mother would find out about him being in jail.

He could also could hear Vick, the boy he was riding with crying a sob story to the police. "It's mine, officer, please lemme go. I promise I won't do it again," whimpered Vick.

"You should of thought of that before you did it," replied the Officer.

Vick was still crying uncontrollable. The police was being tough on a scared straight type tactic, but Luck didn't care. All he wanted was his phone call. *Time to face the music,* Luck thought. "Guard! Gimme my phone call!" Luck screamed.

One of the Police turns towards Luck's direction telling him to "Pipe down in dere! We ain't in no rush!"

Luck gives the officer a killer stare which agitated the cop even more.

"You got a problem!" yelled the Officer. Trying to regain control of the situation.

"Whateva, jus gimme my phone call you clown!" blasted Luck. Flashing a light smirk on his face. "You can't do nuttin' anyway!" he added.

The officer looks in frustration, knowing he wanted to put his hands on Luck but knowing that Luck was right. He couldn't touch Luck at all. The officer unlocks and snatches the cell door open. "Get out and make your call," he said. Luck breezes pass to the cop and head towards the phone on the desk. He picks up the receiver and proceeded to dial his house number.

Ring. Ring. Ring. No answer. *Shit,* thought Luck as he hung up and attempted to dial again. The phone rang out. Again, no answer. His mother must've still been at work or hanging out. He thought.

The officer starts to chuckle soon as he sees that Luck wasn't getting a response from the opposite end.

"What's so funny?" screamed Luck.

"Aww, mommy not comin' to get you? Guess it's Boys village fo' you," answered the Officer. Luck stops in tracks to register what the cop was saying to him.

Boys village? Isn't dat da juvenile detention center for teenagers? pondered Luck. Instantly his mind springs into action. *I can call Pops, he'll come scoop me fo sho,* he thought.

Luck picks the phone back up and dials Pops. Ring. Ring. "Hellooo," answered Pops. Using a scruffy voice like he had just been woken up.

"Pops!" screamed Luck. "Now before you get mad, can you come pick me up from the police station? I'm locked up. I'm not being charged wit nuttin. Please, can you come get me!" he cried.

"What? Boyyy, I should leave yo' ass in there, especially wakin' me up outta my sleep wit dis nonsense, psst! I'm on my way you fuckin dummy!" replied Pops.

More angry now that he had to get out of bed and drive across town to pick up him up. Pops hangs the phone up on Luck without giving him a chance to respond back. That's how he could tell Pops was furious, but nevertheless, he was about to be released so that was a good thing, but still a waiting game until Pops got there.

"I kno" not to ride wit dis dumbass nigga again, psst," Luck said to himself. Then the fact dawned on him that he had missed the get together with Graph and Pooh. "Ahh, shit!" he screamed now feeling riddled with guilt. "I gotta let niggas kno" what happened," he said to himself. "I hope everything went smoothly, no doubt," trying to reassure himself that everything was going to okay. It felt like the time stood still while Luck sat in the cell. He watched as they prepped Vick for transportation down to Boys village.

Luck could see Vick was still sobbing with tears down his cheeks trying to stop his crying dry heaving, trying to catch his breath. "Damn homie!" went Luck, screaming from his cell. Feeling a little pity to see Vick getting hassled and roped up like cattle herd. Wasn't a high profile case but it damn sure felt like it. With the bright lights and mugshot flashings, it made you feel popular but not in a good sense. Luck felt even more antsy knowing he was being released, but the anxiety of when was killing him. "I need to get da fuck outta here!" he cried to himself.

Luck was going bonkers in his mind asking himself questions then answering himself making it more impossible for him to think. Time heal all wounds no doubt, but this time here, was killing Luck's mental. Patience is a virtue but none really took heed to it. Always in a rush to get life done without taking the proper precautions. Is this what you want to be or where? Jail? A convict? Or a criminal? You never really got the choice even though you thought you would because sometimes you were tossed into the wilderness to learn on your own, not knowing what's to become of you.

CHAPTER 6

For the Love

Pooh hops out the cab and heads toward Tawana's house right after he stashed the goods. His stash spot was around by da overpass surrounded by vacant buildings, the perfect spot to hide a needle in a haystack.

Tawana's mother worked the graveyard shift, and Pooh knew he work schedule like clockwork. It's 5:45 a.m., Pooh took more time than he expected to. With all the running around and errands he had to take care of, he was late getting to his girl's house. He taps on the back window lightly, not trying rapture it too hard. After a few taps, Tawana comes to the window.

"Hey, babe," whispered Pooh. "Unlock the back door," he added.

Still wiping her eyes not fully aware yet, she nods her head okay and disappears from the curtains. Pooh goes for the back door when he hears the locks pop.

Tawana cracks the door slightly exposing a little part of her nighty, trying to hide behind the floor from the cold chill that was seeping thru.

"Hey, bae! Hurry up it's cold out here!" she screamed while shivering in her stance.

Pooh slides pass her giving her a kiss on the cheek. "Thanks mama!" he said walking in her house grabbing some warmth. He heads toward her room while she shut and locked the door behind them.

Getting comfortable on her bed, she walks in saying, "Where you been boo? I've been waiting on you since three o'clock this morning to get here. You took so long I fell asleep on yo, ass," saying all this while still yawning, and her eyes half wide open.

"Sorry, baby. Money called, you kno' how dat goes," answered Pooh. Pulling out a wad of money to show it was evidence to what he was saying.

"Ohh, okay. Dat betta be da only thing thats callin you!" returned Tawana, being sarcastic with her response because Pooh stumbled her with the money flash. Pooh lets out a laugh in enjoyment, being intrigued on the fact Tawana had a jealous streak about him.

"Calm down, baby. You kno' you the Bonnie to my Clyde," he said. Handing her the money wad he had on him telling her to put it up.

He normally trusted Tawana with his money, I mean, he couldn't keep it at his house. If his mom found it, she would have a spasm. He couldn't keep it with the stash, that was a no-no, just in case if one got jammed up, it was still options for a comeback. Don't keep the money and drugs in the same spot was a rule; and anybody else he thought about trusting his money with, forget about it. It was a cold world and anyone is capable of taking you off this planet so the only person left was Tawana. Pooh figured as long as she went shopping time to time she wouldn't be a burden on his money.

As she's putting the money up, she said to Pooh, "Me and Malisha are rockin deez stonewashed jean skirts wit da matching tops for da homecoming party. My top is black and hers is blue, but they sho is cute," she boasted.

"Oh yea!" screamed Pooh looking in amusement.

"Oh yea!" she replied back while grabbing the bag from out the closet to show him the outfit. Pooh sees the insignia on the bag. *Rachel's*, a hot topic store in the mall for the females to shop at. She pulls out the ensemble and lays it against her body trying to give Pooh the visual of how it would look on her.

"Ouch!" screamed Pooh. "Y'all gonna be killin dem bitches!" he added.

"Dats da idea!" Tawana chuckles. Adamant about being one of the flyest chicks for the homecoming party.

"Dat shit is fiyah! Real shit!" Pooh spats still analyzing the outfit up and down.

"Thanks, baby. I thought you would love it," she responded. Giving Pooh a kiss on the lips, she turns and put the outfit back up in her closet.

It's 6:15 a.m. It was early, early enough to where you could start hearing the birds chirp. Tawana grabs her towel and robe from off the closet door so she could get ready for her shower. Pooh was lying across her bed watching her get ready. She already started the shower just to get the right temperature for the water. Pooh was getting excited as he watched her get undressed, especially in his pants. A storm was brewing inside him that was about to be released, as he watched Tawana switch her hips towards the bathroom. Pooh was stalking his prey, like animal kingdom ready to pounce on Tawana. He followed behind her unnoticed, sneaking up at the right moment before she disrobed in the bathroom. The bathroom was foggy by the time they both were in there. Pooh planted a kiss on the back of her neck, shaking her knees instantly.

"Ooo, dats my spot. You gon' start dis before I go to school," went Tawana in a low orgasmic voice. Pooh went even harder now, knowing he had Tawana in his clutches. A couple nibbles and bites to arouse Tawana, sucking and tonguing her body like it was his favorite meal. Tawana was puddy in his hands, letting Pooh take control of her. Submissively pressing her against the shower wall, stroking her pleasurably.

"Unnnhh!" she moaned as Pooh goes deeper inside her. The water splashing on them like they were standing underneath a waterfall. Picture somewhere beautiful, tantalizing, and tantric. A standstill type of moment. Their bodies connected like a yin and yang symbol. In and out of each other's spirits like swimming in a sea of eternity. "I love you!"

CHAPTER 7

Everything's a Go!

The birds was chirping as daylight broke the block's horizon. Rizz and Jay had been out since they left the party earlier that night still waiting on Graph anxiously.

"Where da fuck dis nigga at," cried Rizz, looking up and down the street. "Psst! Dis nigga takin all mufuckin day!" he added. Jay just stood in silence while Rizz ranted.

Soon in the distance, Rizz could spot headlights coming from up the street towards their direction.

"Who da fuck is dis comin, bro?" blasted Rizz. "Could be da jakes," he added.

"Shit, I don't kno" but if it is dem boys. I'm skidaddlin! I'm dirty plus got da burner on me, my nigga," returned Jay.

"Da fuck you think imma do, jus' stand here? Nigga, I'm out too!" Rizz screamed while trying to get a better look at the car that was approaching.

The car crept slowly down the street like it was gliding. The moment it got closer, the two could see it wasn't the police but a minivan nearing. Still on a cautious tip, they kept their eyes glued to the vehicle trying to see who it was. They knew no soccer moms was out at this time of the early day.

"Who da fuck is dis pullin up?" went Rizz. Looking cautious, keeping his hand close to his waistband just in case he had to reach.

Jay was already under his shirt by time the van stopped in front of them. The window rolls down.

"Yo, get in!" the voice screamed.

Rizz bending down to get a better look of the driver then realizing that it is was Graph.

"Hurry up, it's hot out here! Jus' seen da boys fuckin wit Roach and Blue around da corner," blurted Graph.

The two hop in the van with Graph then skate. Taillights disappearing into the night.

"Yo, where we headed, cuz?" asked Rizz.

"Southside, I got somethings lined up out dere!" answered Graph.

Rizz sits for a second in deep thought. "South side, ain't dat where Black and dem pump at?" he said to himself. But needless to say, that didn't bother him one bit 'cause Rizz knew he was about any action. They bleed. We bleed. It's all the same in his eyes.

"Okay, you sure dats a good idea, fam? Don't wanna fuck some shit up!" Rizz finally answered. Jay was in the backseat rolling up a blunt eavesdropping to the conversation up front.

"We good, bro, don't worry; and I got somethin' nice fo' y'all" went Graph while turning the steering wheel. He bends the corner into the apartment complex called the "Island views," a spot where Black and his squad set up shop at. Real heavy in these parts of the city. A young nigga, maybe a little older than Graph, and them but a go-getter for his. Didn't make any sense why Graph wanted to post up in this section of the city when he already had two-fourth of it locked down. The east side and the west side was in pocket already, going to war with Black was foolish. Not saying that Graph didn't have the manpower, it just would be bad for business and the city also. Too many casualties at the price of greed wasn't good at all.

Graph pulls up to the apartment building number 1442. He had a crib on the low in the building nobody had knew about. Setting it up on the low because if he had told his niggas, they would've been against it and talked him out of it.

"We're here," went Graph while shutting the car off. Everyone piles out the van stretching. Scouring the scenery, they could spot a group of niggas huddled in front of the building across the court from them. The fellas paid them no mind and headed in the building. As they reached Graph's apartment door, he goes to unlock, that's when his neighbor Melanie pops her head out the door.

It was like she could sense his presence, but in reality, she could hear his keys jingling.

Hey, G, you holdin!" she said.

"Bitch, what I tell you about dat?"

"To page me right, stop wit dis bullshit! You wait 'til I'm … I'm done doin' what I'm doin'!" graph blasted.

You could see the shame fill up in Melanie's face, getting red instantly. Slowly, she dips her head back into her apartment like a turtle retreating into its shell.

The fellas walk in the door, Graph feeling for the light switch soon as he walked in. "Click!" The room brightens up exposing the decorations of the apartment. A fish tank, a big screen TV, and a sectional filled the living room area. Graph heads to the pantry closet next to the kitchen doorway. He pulls out a back bag, turns to Rizz, and tosses it at him. Rizz catches and unzips the bag taking a look inside. His eyes light up.

"Word!" screamed Rizz, bouncing his head like a music tune had just invaded his mind. Getting too hyped and amped up, he shows Jay what was inside the bag. Jay's eyes went double the size they normally were.

"That's fo' you, my nig, told you I wasn't gon' forget about you," went Graph. He was pouring a shot of E & J by the time the two was taking a sneak peek in the bag.

"Bet, my nigga, bet!" returned Rizz, "but I need dat back asap tho, gotta hit da connect back wit his bread, Aight?" added Graph.

"You got it, bro. We 'bout jam off!" finished Rizz.

It was two hundred and fifty grams of snow in the book bag, more than enough to keep these two wolves fed 'til the next plate arrived. The first wave of plans was in motion. The trio sits back, lights up, and start smoking like chimneys, exhaling the smoke like it was a relief off of life.

Now all Graph had to do now was put everyone else in place to start getting this money. The takeover was real in his mind for the fact that the bigger the weight, the bigger the space he was going to need. Expansion was inevitable at some point really, and he felt he needed to do everything necessary to make sure things went smoothly or shit could get catastrophic. Only time would tell.

CHAPTER 8

Hot Seat

"Boy, I'm disappointed in you!" screamed Pops as him and Luck walked in the door.

"But Pop I didddn't do—"

"Shut up!" he said interrupting Luck's side of the story. "Smack!" Pop's hand swiftly catches contact to the back of Luck's head, jerking him forward stumbling. "I don't wanna hear dat shit! You got me outta bed dis late at night. What da hell was you thinkin' about huh?" Pops rambled on. "Pow!" Another slap upside Luck's head.

After Luck regains his balance, he stands in place not saying a word just holding the spot where he just got hit at. After seeing Luck didn't have a response to the question, Pops asked him, he screams, "Get da fuck outta my face! Before I really hurt you."

Luck heads upstairs towards the spare bedroom where he spend the weekends at when he's there staying the night. Sitting on his bedside rubbing the soon to be sore spot on his head, his half-brother Mason slips in his room unnoticed after the commotion.

"What da hell you was thinkin' 'bout, lil bro?" went Mason. Being concerned and nosey at the same time.

"Man bro, it's not even what you think. I didn't get charged wit nuttin and Pops trippin fo' what?" cried Luck.

"Dat nigga trippin' cuz he had to pick yo ass up from the station. What you mean?" returned Mason, trying to be the big brother giving Luck retrospect to why Pops was tripping.

"Yea, you right, bro. I should've jus hopped in a cab," whined Luck.

"Yea, you buggin cuz we don't need no heat and especially you. Don't think I don't kno" what you doin' out dere in dem streets," added Mason. "Jus' be smart, dis chess not checkers, bro," he finished.

"Love, bro," ended Luck. Thanking his brother for the advice, Mason gives him a dap and slips back out the door.

After Mason leaves out the room, Luck decides to blow off some frustration. Already pissed at the fact that he was detained and couldn't make the meeting with Pooh and Graph, thinking them niggas might be mad 'cause he was a no-show.

"Damn, I hope deez niggas ain't heated," he said to himself.

Finally getting the time to cut his pager on, he notices the missed pages from Pooh and a few other people. Luck reaches for the phone and pages Pooh just to let him know he was alive. Late as hell but still in all alive. After doing so, Luck turns on his "Sega Genesis" game. The TV rings with the "Streets of Rage" theme music and the computerized sound effects. A surge of energy rushes thru Luck's body for he knew he was about to release vengeance on the video game. Pressing every button with force as if he was doing the striking himself in the video game. Every hit felt greater than the next. By the blink of an eye, Luck ran thru each level quickly, not noticing he soon finished the game. His frustration blinded his eye for time. He thought by this time Pooh would've been hit him back, unless he was sleep or with a chick. "Fuck it!" he said to himself. "Might as well get some sleep, it's been a long day." Stretching out across his bed, 5:56 a.m. *I'll catch up wit 'em later today,* he thought. Yawning and pass tired, Luck dozes off with ease like a newborn.

It was only but a few minutes 'til Luck was woken up by the door slamming shut. It was his mother who had come, barging into the room waking him up, cursing and hailing up a storm. She was going so fast that Luck couldn't keep up with her but took the lashes long with the verbal bruising.

"Wait 'til we get home!" That's all she kept saying. "Jus' wait!"

The tension and suspense was worse than a horror film, seeing that Luck felt like he was about to be crucified.

Everybody is trippin', what fo'? thinks Luck. Something was a miss except for the shots that was being thrown at Luck that night. A punching bag at its finest! "What a day! What a day!"

CHAPTER 9

Rest, Relaxation, and Recollection

Pooh rolls over in the bed taking a look at the clock on Tawana's nightstand. Still in her house while she was at school, he stayed to take a quick nap. It's 9:15 a.m., Tawana's mother shift ended at ten, giving Pooh enough time to evade the house undetected. While Pooh was getting dressed, grabbing his belongings, he takes a look at his pager and sees a missed page from Luck with the code number 4549. A code that meant ASAP spelled backwards, if you deciphered the numbers. Quickly Pooh grabs the phone dialing the number Luck hit him from.

Ring. Ring.

"Hello," answered Luck in a depressive voice.

"Yo, what's good? You aight? What da fuck happened to you last night?" responded Pooh. An urgency in his voice to get down to the matter of Luck's disappearance.

"Maannn! Fuckin wit dis nigga Vick, bro," cried Luck. "Ridin' wit dis nigga, and he was dirty, got us yanked!" he added. "Luckily I wasn't dirty tho. They lemme go, but dey sent Vick down to BV."

Pooh sits in silence, stunned by the fact of the story he was hearing. Soon, he recollected his words and thoughts.

"Damn, bro, say word. Dats fucked up!" Pooh said.

"At least you were clean tho, shit coulda been worse, ya kno'," he added.

"Yea, true, but mom dukes and pops trippin' hard tho. I been up all night gettin screamed at by them two," cried Luck.

"What da fuck you expect them to do? Your peoples are bonkers!" went Pooh laughing into the speaker while saying this, trying to soften up Luck's blow.

"Yea, I kno', I kno'. But fuck allat! How'd shit flow last night? Smoothly I hope," blurted Luck.

"Yea, we in motion don't worry. I'll be by later to come scoop you, aight?" finished Pooh.

"Aight, bet!" screamed Luck, getting geeked up now from finally hearing some good news after the night he done had.

"I'll be thru after school lets out so dat way nobody's da wiser," added Pooh.

"Aight, I'll be here. I ain't go to school neither. Dey kept me home today because of dat dumb shit last night," went Luck, reassuring Pooh that he was going to be in the house so no more mishaps could happen for him.

"Aight, I'll hit you later, my nig, right befo' I come," replied Pooh.

"Fo sho," ended Luck.

The phone hangs up. Pooh finishes getting his belongings together and exits out Tawana's house. Before doing so, he scour the room one last time, making sure that everything was in place the same way it was when he came in. Pooh exits the house out the back door not to be seen by the neighbors. He had arranged to meet up with Graph at Buzzy's, a home-style fast food place that sat right next to the bodega Mr. Midz. The fellas would go in there just to hang out, grab some grub and play the video arcade games. Pooh had one of Buzzy's specialty-breakfast sandwiches in mind. A sausage, egg, and bacon towered breakfast sandwich topped with Welch's grape jelly.

"Ooowweee!" Pooh screamed to himself, making him more hungry, the more and more he thought about it. Taking more haste in his strides to make it to Buzzy's quicker.

Pooh headed towards the block where the stores sat on. He could see a few people strolling the streets in the early morning. Folks who was walking their children to school to owners opening up their shops. As Pooh was getting closer, he could see Mammie Lay opening up Buzzy's. He was the owner. Soon as the security gates opened, the people that was outside waiting flooded the shop.

Soon as Pooh got in the store, he went towards the arcade games and hit the surge protector.

"He's on fire!" echoes the room from the video games. It was NBA Jams, one of our favorite animated basketball games, filled with theatrics of flaming basketballs and high flying dunks. The fellas stayed on the game like it was nothing, for the gambling and bragging rights of who was the best player throughout the neighborhood.

Pooh screams his order to Mammie while he popped some change into the game.

Soon after, he put his money in the machine, in come walking the rest of the fellas. Graph, Rizz, and Jay. They could sense the food plus the competition easy.

"Da usual!" they screamed as they walked in.

Noticing that Pooh just started the game, Graph yelled "Bet a bill!" Meaning, to bet a hundred dollars to play him.

Pooh casually takes the bet while the other two sit in the back booth and wait.

"He's heating up!" echoed the shop. They played the game intensely, shaking the floor underneath them.

"Is it da shoes?" again goes the machine. After a while, you heard the game-over horn, and that's when you see Pooh was the victor holding his hands up like he won the title bout.

"Ahh, nigga, run dat shit back! You got lucky on dat one!" blasted Graph.

Pooh nods in a sarcastic type gesture, displaying that Graph was no match for him. Agitating Graph a little bit more, he yells, "Double or nuttin, nigga!" Pooh agrees while breaking change for a dollar. He pops the coins in, and they began to play again, and the same results happened. Pooh busted Graph's ass again.

"Fuck allat. What's good wit u?" went Graph. "You ever get dat taken care of?" he added.

"Yea, everything's good. I had Zue spread dat out, jus waitin on them to get rid of it," answered Pooh.

"Okay, dats good. Whatabout Luck tho? You finally get up wit dat nigga?" Graph blurted.

"Oh yea, dat dumb ass nigga got yanked wit Vick last night, but he's home tho. He's good, but Vick got sent to Boys village," Pooh answered.

"Damn, did dey? I kno' da boys was out hot last night when I came to get Rizz and Jay. Maybe dey got caught up in da crosshairs," said Graph.

"Lucky for dat, nigga. Luck tho, he wasn't dirty," he added.

"Yea, I told him the same thing. Imma scoop 'em up after school is over wit and get his portion to him," ended Pooh.

"Yea, we need to get dis shit rollin'. We on a deadline so no fuck ups from here on out, or our necks is on the line, especially mine!" ended Graph.

They look at the clock at the same time, 10:45 a.m.

"Orders up!" screamed Mammie as he lays the food trays on the counter waiting to be picked up. The four grab their food and head back for the last booth in the shop. Right before they all sit down, Graph's beeper goes off frantically. Someone was paging him back to back like it was an urgent matter, but he didn't know the number that was coming across the screen. He sits his food on the table and goes for the payphone. Dialing the unrecognized number, a voice answers on the receiving side.

"Yooo!"

"Who's dis?" went Graph.

"Yo, it's Vito, nigga!" finally Graph catching the voice thru the excitement of Vito's tone.

"Oh, shit! What's good? You blowin' my shit up!" replied Graph.

"Yo, you ain't hear? Black and dem Island niggas got hit last night," blasted Vito.

"Naaahh, I didn't say word!" answered Graph. For a gut feeling of guilt hits him, knowing he was on that side of town last night. Graph didn't have nothing to do with the robbery 'cause Rizz and Jay could vouch that, but who would've took their word for it, knowing how them "WP boys" got down. Graph's focus now was on him being implemented in the heist, a misconception rather.

"You be careful, bro. Dem niggas is on da hunt. One of dem niggas shot Black too," added Vito. "Might think we had somethin' to do wit it. I don't kno"; but either way, keep your eyes peeled, son!" he finished.

The three at the table could see how the face of confusion came across Graph while he was on the phone. Graph became uneasy while talking to Vito the fellas could notice.

"Aight, good look, fam. You be safe and lemme kno' if you hear anythin' else," ended Graph before he hung the phone up.

Graph sits down in the booth, wiping his face out of confusion.

"Who was dat, bro?" went the table all at once, being nosey to why Graph's whole demeanor changed.

"Dat was Vito!" answered Graph.

"What da fuck he wanted?" cried Pooh.

"He was jus' tellin me, Black and his boys got hit last night; and one of dem niggas popped Black in da mix," went Graph while shaking his head like he was trying to get something out.

"Damn. Are you serious!" blasted Pooh. "Who? How?" he added.

"Don't kno' who, dats why Vito said be on da lookout. No one knows who pulled da strings. Dey could think we had something to do wit it, ya kno'," finished Graph.

The feeling sets in Graph more as if he was guilty because he put himself in a position where he could be tied to the robbery just by being in that part of town at that time. He knew Rizz and Jay wouldn't say nothing. Them, two didn't give two fucks of who thought what. Pooh was the only one that was out the loop about Graph's secret bando, and he would trip if he found out.

"Jus' send da word out to be on guard, Aight?" ended Graph.

"You got dat, big bro, say no mo!" returned Pooh.

The rest of the table nodded their heads in agreement. If they fuck with one of us, they damn sure fucking with all of us. Soon after the four rallied up, they went back to devouring their breakfast that was smelling all so good. *Heaven on a plate*, they thought, especially when you're dealing with the munchies!

CHAPTER 10

Lost time made for

"Time to punch da clock," Luck said to himself while pacing impatiently back and forth in his room. Waiting for Pooh's arrival, anxiously ready to get out the house he been sitting in.

All day he was going stir crazy and missing money. His pager was full from all the beeps he was getting. A few from Manny and Blake, and the rest was from his customers.

"Damn dis nigga need to hurry up," he said again to himself. "Mufucka's waitin' on me, and I can't do nuttin 'til dis nigga get here, psst." Still thinking and impatient, Luck had no choice but to wait. It was his fault for not being at the meeting last night so he couldn't complain about Pooh taking his time. Moments later, he hears a car horn going off out front.

"Beep! Beep!"

The anxiety in Luck evaporated once he heard the horn. "Thank God!" he screamed.

Grabbing his jacket and keys bolting for the door. Soon as he stepped out on the porch, he threw his hands up like he was a free man.

"What up, cuzzo?" Luck screamed to Pooh from a distance as he was approaching the car to get in. Pooh chuckles by the antics Luck was portraying, like he was a convict who had been incarcerated most of his life.

"What's da deal?" went Pooh.

Luck gets settled in the car before giving Pooh a dap.

"Ain't shit ready to get dis money, ya heard!" cried Luck.

"Bet dats what I like to hear," Pooh returned.

The car pulls out of the cul-de-sac where Luck lived in. They headed towards "Da Greens" where Luck normally posted up at.

"Yea, I got da fellas waitin'. Errythin lined up, fam," blurted Luck.

"Aight, dats sounds like a plan, jus' make it happen captain!" Pooh replied.

The car pulls into the roundabout that surrounded "Da Greens." Pooh and Luck could see Manny, Blake, and OJ standing in front of the buildings, posted like mailboxes, hungry these fellas were and looked. No time for games, niggas were out ready to eat and plunder. Pooh pulls the car into a spot, throwing the gear into park. He reaches in the backseat and grabs a bag, giving it to Luck.

"Hunh, here you go!" said Pooh.

Luck didn't open it because he already knew what was inside of it.

"Bet, my nigga, imma jam dis ASAP!" he screamed.

Now more excited that he received what he'd been waiting for.

"Yea, we need dat bread pronto. Da connect only gave us two weeks so no fuck ups, bro!" went Pooh.

"Oh, no worries my, nig. We got dis," claimed Luck.

"Good. When you're done, you know what to do and how to do it. Jus like we explained befo', Aight?" Pooh said.

"Say no mo'!" screamed Luck while exiting out of the car.

"Hold up! Befo' I forget, Black and them got hit last night. Don't kno" by who tho, but be safe 'cause you kno" niggas can get da wrong ideas."

"Damn, you forreal!" blasted Luck hanging halfway out the car, listening to the bombshell that was just dropped in his lap.

"Yea, so jus' stay low, and let's get dis bread," ended Pooh.

"Fo' sho!" ended Luck while finally exiting the car fully.

Pooh backs up and pulls off leaving Luck in his rear view. Luck was still standing looking at Pooh drive off into the wind still pondering on what he had just heard. Stuck in a daze.

Black? How? Who could get dat close to 'em? Luck thought. His mind raced with multiple questions until Manny broke his concentration by saying, "Yoo! We good!"

Luck snaps back to the matter at hand getting this money.

"Yea, we good, jus' be on the lookout if any of dem Island niggas come thru here. Aight?" Luck answered. "Don't kno" if we got a situation or not, but let's jus' be careful of it," he added.

"You already kno"," returned Manny. "Now what's up wit da work, we good?" he added.

Luck shows him the bag, holding it up. "Dinners right here, nigga!" he boasted. The whole squad grinned like "The Grinch who stole Christmas."

"Let's eat!" agreed the fellas. The rest can say their prayers now, for it was feasting time.

"Amen!"

CHAPTER 11

The Story of Kato

"It's all about the Benjamins, baby!"

The money started flowing like a levee had broken. It was a glorious time, especially when you had food on the table to eat.

Everyone had a dollar or two in their pockets. When the block was operating at a decent rate, you would be a fuck up not to come up.

The whole operation was running smoothly, with Graph holding Washington park down. Pooh was controlling the westside and Luck had "Da Greens" rolling. A perfect trifecta with a little sprinkles here and there. The squads was eating, moving mass quantities of cocaine throughout the city undetected.

You could tell niggas was getting paid by the looks of it. New clothes draped their bodies. Some wore matching kicks to rep their neighborhood blocks, all different types of flavors like a bag of skittles. Others started sporting jewelry, such as chains, watches, and bracelets, even gold teeth became epidemic. When Wu-tang dropped, and everyone seen the gold fangs, it was a must that we had to have them. Fashion stocks damn sure spiked up around this time. Everyone was flooding the malls frequently.

A beautiful time to floss on your haters, which more than likely you would have when you accumulated some change.

Now, how things normally go when you become a little notice in the game. You start to hear the stories of the people who came before you. The four father in the game. One in fact was the story of *Kato*.

Now Kato was an old school cat somewhere from down south, nobody really knew where. He was the next original connection to the cocaine flow as far as some could remember, pushing heavy weight in these streets before our early days.

Kato ruled with an iron fist after the first trio of legends dissipated, not playing no games about his business. He was an arrogant, pompous type of cat, ignorant to everyone except his money. Most would hang around him just for the reason he was getting money and flashy. Sometimes he even kept some of the young fellas around for quick store errands and also to bully or haze, ridicule even.

Dice games would be the stage for such theatrics. When someone is the victim of getting their money took by gambling was no thrill. Competition was inevitable, but losing your money was devastating, and the worse time to lose your money was when you used your re-up for a come up. That's when shit could go sideways and become intense, leaving the situation in a critical state.

One particular day, the stage was set, where Kato was rolling the dice, and Graph was fading him. At this time, Graph was up and coming, making a little change on the side with Rizz and Jay doing some home burglaries, who also had happened to be present at the dice game.

"Head crack!" went Kato as the dice lands on seven, picking up the money he just won. Graph throws some more money down on the ground.

"Bet it back!" he screamed.

Getting more frustrated and anxious 'cause he could see his money was getting low. Kato shakes the dice up, blow them, then rolls them. They land on eleven this time.

"Strike 'em!" screamed Kato, laughing while picking up the money. "I'm hot, lil nigga. You betta watch it!" Kato added.

Without hesitation and thought, Graph throws down what he had left in his hand. "Send me home!" blasted Graph, hoping that Kato would crap out and he could get a chance at a hot streak; but it didn't happen that way.

"Seven again!" went Kato.

This nigga must've just came from Las Vegas. The way his wrist was on fire. Graph sat in a trance for a second looking at the dice. Kato's laugh soon sparked the anger inside of Graph as he throws the dice then snatches the money.

"Nah, nigga. You cheatin'!" screamed Graph. "What da fuck you think dis is?"

Kato don't say anything but instantly swings, catching Graph's jaw. Stumbling him back a few steps, Kato tries to go in for another punch, and that's when Rizz grabs a hold of him from behind.

"Get off me, lil nigga!" Kato screamed as he wiggles out the arms of Rizz.

Gaining enough distance from the trio, Kato draws out from his waistband exposing his 45 caliber pistol.

"I should bust yo shit wide, nigga!" he screamed walking up on Graph placing the barrel underneath his chin. Rizz and Jay just freeze in their tracks.

"You got dat, big homie. You got it," whined Graph.

"Fuck, you think dis a game huh?" blurted Kato. "Get your weight up and not your hate up, nigga!" he finished.

Tossing an eight ball of coke down on the ground and putting his gun back in his waistline, Kato steps off casually; but before doing so, he screams back at Graph, "Holla at me when you finish dat, lil nigga!" Trying to add insult to injury with saying this. He disappears thru the project buildings.

Soon as the three were alone, they all looked at each other not saying a word. Yup, each one knew what the other was thinking, telepathically reading one another's mind. *Dis nigga gotta go!* they thought, and what better way to get revenge was to serve it on a cold dish; but in this case, they had something hot for Kato's ass.

Now time went pass, and things was forgot about, well for Kato that was. Graph still had a score to settle with this nigga for the disrespect of putting his hands on him. Graph didn't allow nobody to touch him, only one that got away with it was his big brother, and still he didn't approve of it.

Now the plan was to have Jay set the buy up from Kato, luring him to the boardwalk where Rizz and Graph would be waiting. That's where Kato's resting place would be, and to top it off with a cherry, they would swindle a brick out the ordeal. How to lure Kato out was money. He was blinded by greed so Jay had fabricated to Kato that he wanted to grab a brick from him. Jay had seen Kato earlier that day with one of his homies that he didn't know. Still setting the plan up, Kato said he'd be there.

Now, nobody knows what really happened, seeing that no one witnessed it. All the city knew was Kato suddenly came to a quick demise. Tragic for some, and others thought a relief; therefore, the streets were open for the taking now. A 50/50 if you will. The cops found Kato's body washed up off the shoreline naked with three bullets in his head.

Rumors started to float around the city about who clipped Kato. One rumor that could've held water was the one they had about Graph. Reason being, the streets thought he had something to do with the expiration of Kato, was one. Graph came up with more weight than he normally had, raising suspicion of where he had got it from; and two, was when the cops found Kato's body, They said he was naked, but they found drugs on him, an eight ball shoved in his mouth. Coincidental or ironic huh? Let the streets be the judge of that!

CHAPTER 12

All Good just a Week Ago

It was all good just a week ago, or nothing good lasts forever at some point.

Somewhere, the hamster fell off the wheel meaning that something was in the air, and everyone involved could feel it. Getting closer to the homecoming, relationships got intense. The rivalry game was the highlight of the year, and everyone whose someone was going to be attending. The Eagles versus the Rams, a battle that was similar to the Hatfields and Mccoy's—a real shootout on the playing fields both ways.

Zue was nervously pacing back and forth, smoking cigarette after cigarette, exhaling the smoke with haste. "What da fuck?" he said to himself.

Looking at the fresh batch they received and just finished cooking. The product came up short. The last shipment did the same thing but not as much as the one they had now. They lost big on this one. Ten thousand grams was no light work. Now wasn't the time for a hick up. The well in the streets would run dry, and people will start to look for new places to drink, bad for business at its worse.

All why thinking this, Zue was waiting for the phone to ring. He paged Pooh as soon as he finished with the work.

"Dis nigga ain't gon' believe dis shit here," Zue said to himself while double-checking the weight.

A few seconds goes pass then the phone rings. "Hello," went Pooh.

"Yoo! We got a situation over here! You need to come check dis out ASAP!" rambled Zue.

"What? Wait, what's goin' on?" cried Pooh.

"That bowl of punch been spiked, dats what goin' on, nigga!" answered Zue.

"Hold up, you serious? How much?" Pooh asked.

You could tell he was excited by the elevation in his voice. The two was having a verbal match. "Like ten liters, bro!" answered Zue.

"You sure, nigga? You sure you ain't do nuttin to it?" said Pooh.

"Nigga, you kno' me! How dat sound?" screamed Zue. "You know how I get down! We been rockin too long for me to bite the hands that's feeding us, c'mon, son!"

Pooh goes silent for a second, feeling a lump of guilt for questioning Zue's loyalty and expertise.

"My bad, bro. I kno' you, my nigga. No harm, no foul, but dis puts a monkey wrench in our program dats fo sho," he goes. "Dats not even enough to pay da connect back with," he added.

"I already kno', bro. Dats why I hit you ASAP to tell you! You gon' have to hit Graph up and tell him to holla at dat nigga to fix dis!" finished Zue.

"Yea, aight, in da mean time, you put up what you have over there up until we figure dis shit out. I'm 'bouta to hit dis nigga now," said Pooh. "I'll be over there in a few. You be easy, bro, one," he ended. They both hang up.

After Pooh hung up with Zue, he dials Graph and waits. While waiting on word from him, his pager goes off.

Beep beep! Beep beep! Number 4549! It wasn't Graph, but instead, Luck was trying to get a hold on him. Pooh seen that it was urgent, so he quickly calls Luck.

"Yo!" went Pooh.

"Yo, my nigga, you not gon' believe dis shit here!" cried Luck.

"What da fuck you talkin' 'bout?" Pooh returned with a rush in his voice for Luck to get straight to the point.

"Da drop got hit last night, nigga! Whoever it was, jammed Blake and OJ at the spot!" Luck screamed. "Dat was da whole kit and kaboodle right dere," he added.

Pooh gets numb all over, not feeling his legs. He sits down.

"Wait, how da fuck dis happen?" he said.

"Niggas tryin' to figure dat out now. OJ said da niggas was in a 96 Buick Lesabre, a burgundy-type color."

The phones go silent briefly. You could tell Pooh was registering what Luck was telling him, doing the calculations in his head.

"A burgundy 96 Buick Lesabre?" he said to himself. "Only person in da city wit dat type of car was Black that he knew of."

"You sure, bro?" Pooh asked.

"Yea, my nigga. I'm lookin' at Blake's eye right now. His shit shinin! Lucky dey ain't getta clappin then niggas really would've been done," answered Luck.

"Yea, you right, but now we gotta find out dis Buick. I think I kno' who it is!" went Pooh.

"Do you? Tell me who you think it is! My niggas ready!" blasted Luck.

"I don't kno' for sure, but I think dats Black's squad. Don't quote me yet tho. Let's jus' figure dis shit out 'cause we have another problem on our hands" blurted Pooh.

"Whats dat?" asked Luck.

"Dat bowl of punch been spiked!" Pooh answered.

"Get da fuck outta here. You serious?" screamed Luck. "And now dat dis happened also, I tell you something's up, cuz!" he ended.

The feeling was in the air that the wind turned in a different direction than what the fellas had expected it to. Conflicts started to arise and so did temperatures. It was about to get hot, and hell was awaiting.

"Yea, so sit tight and don't do nuttin 'til we get some type of word back; but trust we gon' find out who's behind dis shit, bet dat! I'll holla, be safe!" Pooh ended as he hung up. "Wait 'til dis nigga hear da shit goin' on here. He gon' shit a brick!" Pooh was saying to himself as he waited for Graph's phone call so he could relay the bad news to him. That was the worst ever, being the bearer of bad news.

Pooh knew Graph was going to be upset seeing that mishaps started to occur. It was cool if the work had got mixed up because he could manage to get around that, but the drop from Luck's portion was a setback. A two-headed monster, there's the product then there's the money. Both couldn't be in the grinder at the same time, where you need one, you would need the other to get. Just like as if it was bread and butter or peanut butter and jelly, whichever is suitable for whoever. They intertwined with each other.

Pooh was smoking a blunt by time the cab pulled up to get him. Trying to relieve some tension from his brain, the only medicine was the reefer. He didn't believe it was impossible to make the comeback. Pooh was more concerned on how someone could have known where the drop was. Was they following the operation, or was it a leak inside of the camp? *Can't be!* Pooh thought.

The last bit of smoke seeps thru his mouth as he hops in the car. He was going to check Zue out to make sure he wasn't dreaming when it came to the loss on the shipment he was informed about. This wasn't the problems Pooh wanted on his plate, with schoolwork, and Tawana's recent naggings, and now the magnitude of this catastrophe. Pooh felt like he was on the edge trying to keep his empire balanced. This is what CEO's go thru, but the trick was to stand in the fire, and let it burn so you could never feel them flames ever again; and if you seen it coming then you would know how to put it out. Pay attention, breath, and never let them see you sweat or fold. Master the masks of emotions, and disguise your traits so no one could ever read the cards in your hand, always good to have the upper hand even if you had to bluff at times.

CHAPTER 13

Can it be that it was All so Simple then

Can it be that it was all so simple then. Back when no responsibilities mattered but being a kid, keeping up with your chores and grades. That's all that mattered to our parents, was not to get in trouble. The days you were unconscious to the facts and consequences of life.

Graph was addicted to strip clubs, even tho he had a girl. It was a thrill of excitement to see female asses bounce in front of him. He loved to watch them gyrate like an earthquake was happening. It was a rush for him. All different size and talented ladies doing the most seductive and freakish dance acts. He considered it his *house of love*.

"Shake dat ass, guurl!" went Graph, tossing money at the dancer that was performing before him. "Oh, shit! Daaatttsss what I'm talkin' about, bounce dat!" he added.

Flashing his new customized WP gold ring as he threw the money in the air, cutting the lights with his diamonds. Enjoying himself freely and expressing his naughty by nature side. Graph was in bliss.

"Oooh, I like dat dere!" again goes Graph.

The dancer was going into hype mode now that the music tempo changed to a more upbeat rhythm, seeing Graph was getting more interested.

He was having so much fun. He never checked his pager, but his hip kept vibrating. Thinking it was the stripper the whole time dancing on him, he never paid attention.

Finally, he spots the light from his pager going off from out the corner of his eye. He snatches the pager off his hip checking the number, number 4549! Number 911!

It was Pooh trying to reach him urgently. Graph throws the dancer that was sitting in his lap off him. Sending her tumbling to the ground, she screams, "Unnhhh! You asshole!"

Graph didn't pay no attention to her remarks but concentrated on dialing Pooh from his Startec cellphone. "Ring!"

"Yo, nigga, where you been? Been tryna get a hold of you all day!" blasted Pooh thru the phone.

"Why, what's good, nigga? Talk to me!" answered Graph.

"A whole lot, nigga. The shipment is light for one, and Luck and 'em got hit for the drop money fam!" answered Pooh.

"Whattt!" screamed Graph.

The anger inside Graph started brewing up like a hot pot of grits being overcooked.

"What da fuck you mean? What da fuck is goin' on out dere?" added Graph.

Now that Pooh had his undivided attention, he was trying to get down to the bottom of this situation.

"Maannn, look, you need to holla at homie and get dat food straight! Let's worry 'bout dat first. We won't make enough money to pay the connect back," blurted Pooh.

"And whatabout da hit, nigga? What? Niggas supposed to do, jus' let it go? Fuck dat, someone knows somethin. What Luck and dem say 'bout it?" rambled Graph.

"He said somethin' about a Burgundy Buick Lesabre. Da niggas was in. Only person I can think wit one is dat nigga Black!" answered Pooh. "I don't kno' fo sho but it could be dem niggas, heard Black's back around," he added.

The phone goes dead silent, Graph just heard the words he got robbed, not to mention the fact that this is what he feared with Black's retaliation. The streets talk and watch for that matter; and someone was watching and definitely talking, no doubt.

"The shipment was light. The drop got hit, and nobody knew nothing, not yet at least." All the blood was rushing to Graph's brain along with the thoughts he was having.

"Yo, I'm on my way! Have everyone meet me at da overpass in a hour. You got dat?" exclaimed Graph.

"Bet we'll be there, Audi 5000!" ended Pooh. The phone call comes to a screeching end.

The whole time the conversation was going on, the stripper was still standing there cursing Graph out with him, not paying her no mind. Finally turns to her and said, "Bitch hunh, take dis and shut da fuck up!"

Tossing a wad of money big enough to shut her yapping up with. She starts scooping the money up off the ground while Graph stepped over her like the king he thought he was.

And now, it felt like it was time to polish up the Crown once again!

CHAPTER 14

Affirmative Action

Pooh did just like Graph said to, to get everyone grouped at da overpass.

He already told Luck to come, figuring that Graph would tell Rizz and Jay to show up. The rest would get the relayed message to be there. It was around 11:40 p.m. when people started to show up. First to arrive was Roach and Blue since their buildings was the closes to the bridge, next was Luck, Manny, and Blake. You could see OJ towering behind the three as they walked up. Trav and Vito popped out the cut taking a shortcut down the train tracks. So far so good, it looked seeing that everybody got word to make it to da overpass. Later came Pooh with Zue strolling up to the group that was huddled waiting.

"What's da deal, my nig?" went everyone, getting acquainted with each other like they were long lost relatives reuniting.

Pooh answers the squad saying, "Waitin' on dis nigga Graph ta pull up. Some shit don popped off!"

The group listens to Pooh like he was conducting a seminar, investing an interest.

Everyone was standing around looking in bewilderment as to what Pooh was trying to say. A few blunts rotated in the mix forming a cloud over their heads.

Even if you didn't smoke, it was enough to catch second hand from.

Moments went by then, that's when Graph arrived, pulling up in Gerald car. And like Pooh assumed, he had Rizz and Jay with him. The three pile out the car meeting up with the rest of the huddle.

"Yo, what's good, what's good?" went Graph. Walking into the crowd giving everyone dap. "Glad niggas are out. We got shit to handle!" he added.

The crowd began to rile up seeing Graph just implied that something was up, even more when they saw his face was bothered with the problem.

"What's good?" one of the fellas screamed.

"I don't kno', but imma find out!" answered Graph. "Nun of dem Island niggas is allowed out here, ya dig! You see 'em. You crash 'em!" he added.

The crowd got even noisier now, more pumped off an adrenaline boost, ready to mash out and cause some havoc.

A couple of "Hell, yeas!" and "You mufuckin right!" chanted amongst the crowd, showing and confirming that everyone was on the same page.

Out of nowhere, Rizz spitted, "You kno' homecoming is soon, and nine times outta ten dem niggas gon' be in there, right? So what you wanna do?" he finished.

"It's whateva forreal, forreal! Imma rap to dat nigga, but if he pops slick, I'm rockin 'em straight up!" answered Graph.

"Well, fuck it. I got your back either way, doggy!" replied Rizz. "Let dem niggas act up!" he added.

The rest followed the wave like a domino trail. "Fuck dem niggas! Anyone of 'em can get it!"

More rants coming from the crowd now. It felt like they wanted the niggas to pop off so they had reason to fuck some shit up. I mean, they felt like they were the reason their money flow started slowing up, with the drop being grabbed. The work was another thing that Graph had to get straightened out, but still niggas wasn't having it. Still not hearing back from Southern Comfort, he was in a standstill position. He was sitting on five thousand grams when he owed Southern Comfort for ten thousand. Something had to give. *Maybe dis nigga knew what he was doing, I don't kno'*, thought Graph rolling up a blunt, trying to regain his composure and ease his mind. Nevertheless, if Southern Comfort didn't fix it then he would just have to shop for a new outlet.

"Yo, I need y'all two to meet me at La Cafe tomorrow afternoon, aight? It's a new spot on da lower west side," went Graph as he pulls Pooh and Luck off to the side so no one could hear him whisper.

"Yea, I heard about dat spot. Some cubans or mexicans own it, I dunno! But I kno' where it's at," replied Pooh.

Luck confirmed with a head nod because he was choking by this time. The smoke constricting his lungs tightly.

"Aight, fam, don't forget tomorrow," ended Graph. "I'll catch up later!"

The right for ownership was on the line and everyone had to play the frontline, or the chain would break; and all could be lost or astray, so it was a must to protect the dynasty they built.

The crowds disperse in different directions, heading back to the comforts of their natural habitats, *the Streets! Home sweet home;* but some could get lost in this wonderland here!

CHAPTER 15

Love from a Distance

Malisha and Tawana was in the hair salon getting glamoured. The two was getting their hair and nails done for the nearing homecoming party.

Hair salons were the equivalent to barber shops when it came to the gossiping around town. You would and could hear all types of stories floating around inside the four walls of these establishments from the hottest trends to who's cheating on who. It didn't matter because someone was always talking "Girl, we gon' be some of da baddest bitches in da building! You hear me, bish!" spitted Malisha leaning back in the chair next to Tawana relaxing while the people worked on their hands and feet.

"Guurll! Dis is heaven right here!" returned Tawana. "It never gets old, boo!" she added.

"Yea, you right. I could never get tired off dis shit!" boasted Malisha.

They were getting more comfy in the seats as the two conversated, chuckling and laughing as if it wasn't a care in the world.

R & B slow songs was playing throughout the shop, setting the ladies in a serene mood while they were being taking care of. A peaceful state of mind, why they felt to get pampered and treated for once. At least they felt they deserved to, consider the two was holding Graph and Pooh down without a question.

Their loyalty was never in question for the two, knowing that these chicks loved them. They would go to war for their men.

"Aye, bish, did you hear what happened?" blurted Malisha. Leaning over closer to Tawana.

"Nah gurl what?" answered Tawana in a haste to find out the juicy news.

"I heard G and P stash got hit!" Malisha goes.

"How you kno'!" cried Tawana.

"I overheard Graph talkin' to someone about it. I don't who or how much it was, but I kno' dem niggas is pissed, bish!" Malisha answered.

"Gurl, you lyin. I didn't hear nuttin about it," Tawana chimed.

"Of course you didn't. You think dem niggas is gon' tell us, hell nah!" blasted Malisha. "For all dey kno' is we don't kno' nuttin, but bitch I kno'!" she added.

"Do you kno' who had somethin' to do wit it? C'mon, bish, I kno' you kno'!" Tawana asked.

"Nah, not much, somethin' about da Island boys I don't kno' fully," she answered.

"Oh, wow, gurl. I kno' how dem two can get, and dem niggas betta be careful because they fuck wit my bae. It's a problem!" went Tawana.

She was getting antsy from hearing the news that someone was messing with her baby. Tawana wasn't having it nor was Malisha for that matter, but what could they do, they couldn't say anything about it because they weren't supposed to know in the first place. But the fact remained that the news couldn't escape their minds now, so they just hoped the pampering would take the negative energy out their bodies and the room. Tawana had been feeling sick lately thinking with all the stress and schoolwork that was going on. She thought it could've been exhaustion, so she felt this was a great time she could relax with her best friend and relieve some tension and live for the time being. The homecoming was going to be epic, a night to come and a night to remember; but before the girls finished with their beauty transformations, Tawana gets a sick feeling, instantly running to the bathroom to throw up. Leaving Malisha in a stare as to what was wrong with her. She said to herself, "What da fuck wrong wit her! I hope dis bish ain't pregnant!"

CHAPTER 16

Plan B

Rizz and Jay was plotting their own plans to what Graph had arranged. Knowing he didn't want nobody making a move without consent, the two felt it was a must to send a message not to fuck with them.

"Yo, dem Island niggas is throwin a hotel party after da homecoming!" went Jay.

"A lil bitch I been fuckin wit said she was invited!" he added.

"Oh, word!" cried Rizz. "Dem niggas ain't gon' kno" what hit 'em!" he finished, rubbing his hands together like they were two sticks trying to make fire.

You could see the hunger in the two eyes like they lived for these pleasures, to inflict chaos on whoever opposed.

"We need one other person, and it'll go smoothly because we can't let Graph kno'! He'll tell us not to do it!" Jay blurts.

"Man, fuck dat. What's good fo us is good fo Graph! Dat nigga a be aight!" screams Rizz. "Imma get my peoples Malik to come. I kno' he's down!" Rizz added.

"You sure, nigga, he good peoples?" asked Jay.

"Yea, nigga. I wouldn't of mentioned him if he wasn't! He knows da ropes!" blasted Rizz.

"Aight, aight! Well let's hit dem niggas tomorrow night then after da game!" finished Jay.

"It's lined up. Don't worry, we in there!" boasted Rizz.

As the two conversed over the details of hitting Mack's squad tomorrow night, they enjoyed the tranquilities of smoking on some hydro. Hit after hit nonstop, the fellas was floating like a cloud passing thru on a windy day.

"All I kno' is niggas don started something!" went Jay, exhaling the smoke, feeling more anxious now to make that move.

"I'll find out which hotel it is once I holla at shawty, aight?" Jay finished.

It was a good feeling to have the element of surprise on your opponents especially when they wouldn't even expect to see it coming. Thinking everything was peachy keen, but in all, it wasn't. Nobody cared really or paid attention to details. All they ever did was act off of impulse. Not knowing the whole story could hurt your plans, let alone someone's feelings. You can't be gullible to every story you hear. If you don't stand for something, then you can fall for anything; and now wasn't the time for bungee jumping even though shit was about to go down.

And these two were ready for dishing out a little payback for the occurrences they've been having lately. You like to fuck with our money, well it's a must they come fuck with yours. The heat was definitely in the kitchen by this time, and the only question was who was going to manage to take it when shit popped off!

"Bet!" ended Rizz, feeling gratification on the circumstances that was about to take place.

CHAPTER 17

Chess Moves or a Checker Jumps

At 1:25 p.m., the trio finally huddled around a table inside of the restaurant, "La Cafe," a new spanish spot that opened up recently on the west side of the city.

Graph and Pooh was into trying new cuisines time to time just to get the sensation of another's culture. Anywhere from Jamaican to Mexican dishes was an experience for the fellas. Luck was a straight American-style eater, hamburger and fries type of guy, didn't take much to please his fat boy nature.

The trio takes a glance at the menus when the server approached, ordering their drinks first to buy themselves some time before ordering. Once the server left to grab their drinks that's when Graph speaks, "Yo, I rapped to dat nigga Southern Comfort. He told me to come down so he can set shit straight. He said dis shipment to keep as a bonus, and he'll make up for our loses."

Pooh and Luck didn't respond quite yet, just was taking in what Graph was telling them.

Finally, with concern about the ordeal, Pooh asked, "When you gotta do dis!"

"He wants me to be there by tomorrow night. He already has da ticket waitin' at da airport fo' me," answered Graph.

"Damn, son. You kno' the game is tomorrow night, bro. How you gonna swing dat?" cried Pooh.

"Not gonna be able to make it, bro, shit we gotta get dis shit fixed ASAP! What you rather be broke, or lemme go handle dis shit? Which one?" blasted Graph.

You could tell he was a little agitated by Pooh's concern about a party rather than getting their street affairs straightened out.

"Of course let's get dis shit straight. I'm jus' sayin' Malisha gon' be mad at yo ass for not making it!" spitted Pooh.

"Maann, look she'll be aight! Jus' sent dat bitch to da mall yesterday and to da shop. Dat bitch betta shut da hell up fuckin wit me!" Graph boasted.

The server returned with the three's drink, now ready to take their orders. The manager of the cafe was floating around his establishment, being a busy body for one and on the other hand being nosey trying to meet his new customers. Graph chose foreign places to eat and talk at because he felt at ease that no one could hear his conversation or let alone it being understood. The fellas couldn't grab the vibe the manager was giving off. It wasn't a bad vibe nor a good one, more on the lines of who was the manager. Why was he so friendly and eager to meet and greet folks? Where was he from? And why was he trying to get so close? Who knows, but these were all the questions the three was asking themselves about the mysterious foreign guy. Looks Cuban or Mexican; but either way, it was all the same to them, a nigga who couldn't speak a lick of English.

"While I'm gon, I need y'all to handle shit 'til I touch back down, coo?" went Graph. "Da way he was talking, we gon' have to do double time on da next wave! So we should be good on dat time we lost!" he added.

We got dat big homie. no worries, jus' be safe and bring dat food home cuz we hungry!" Laughed Luck.

It was too much anxiety going on with the city at siege, and the well running short of water, so Luck's response was to lighten up the mood. It seemed like no one had smiled or laughed in days seeing that this was a rough patch in their program. Nevertheless, something had to shake or retirement came early for them, and that wasn't an option they planned on taking.

"You kno' it's other connects, bro?" went Pooh. "We don't gotta keep fuckin wit dat dirty south, nigga!" he added.

The manager face lights up out of nowhere like he just won on a lottery ticket. Not really paying attention to the man eavesdropping, the fellas continued on with their convo, giving the nosey manager something he wanted to hear.

"When da time comes for it, we'll do so, 'til then we stuck fo right now, aight?" Graph answered.

"Aight, bro, as long as you kno'," returned Pooh.

Luck wasn't saying anything, just taking everything in a long with the food he was shovelling in his mouth, but coherent to what was being discussed.

"I'll let y'all kno' when I touch down out there," finished Graph.

"Fo sho!" went Luck and Pooh at the same time getting deeper into their meals now. The food took over their focus once the smell hit them. A succulent spicy dish for a spicy topic, where two the coincided with one another, Day and Night.

CHAPTER 18

The Homecoming

Boom! Boom! Clap!
   Boom Boom! Clap!
   The chants were coming from the cheerleaders frantically hyping the crowds up with their theatrics. "You ugly, you, you, you ugly!" Taking shots at each other's opposing team with criticism and rants. The crowd was intense, both sides of the field with the stands vibrating with such force beneath them. Nothing but all mean mugs and shoulder bumps took place, some were accidental and some was intentional, packed like sardines in a can.
   Pooh and the fellas walked into the oval shaped field mobbing like a small mosh pit. Obnoxiously loud and amplified for their home team the Eagles to win the football game tonight was their reason for how they were acting. Rizz was more excited because he was going to see his little brother Harvey play against the rival team. Harvey was the star running back for the Eagles, and Rizz knew he was going for the gold against the Rams to make a highlight reel for the days to come and be forever remembered.
   Anyone who anticipated the game and was attending the event was looking forward to the match-up. The citywide super bowl in the eyes of the people is how they saw it. Reaching and becoming the state champions was the absolute goal for the team, but to beat and humiliate your arch nemesis on the way to that was the icing on

top of the cake. Bragging rights becomes endless when memories of greatness are etched in stone.

Now, while everyone was getting ready for kick-off, finding their seats hasty, Pooh spots Black's little brother John-John across the field with his accompanied crew. He could see that Black was nowhere to be seen on the sidelines with his little brother and the Island boys. You could spot the opposing sides because the Rams wore black and red while the Eagles sported gold and blue.

The atmosphere was pandemonium. The ground was shaking as if the Titans themselves was walking the field.

Helmets cracking and loud banter soon erupted as the kick lifted the football in the air.

"Heeerrreee weee gooo!" went the announcer's voice echoing thru the stadium speakers.

Pooh thought it would be best to wait until halftime to see if Black arrives and then approach him. His intentions was to talk and hash out any differences and assumptions and find a solution to the cause peacefully, if there was a problem to begin with. Not trying to add fuel to a fire, but if you pissed gasoline onto a flame, no telling who would get burned in the process. Now halftime normally is when the fans would head to the concession stands for refreshments and to loiter with friends and family, to stretch your legs and shoot the breeze 'til second half began.

Malisha and Tawana was sitting close to the top of the bleachers with a few of their other chicks. Pooh and the fellas made their way up the stairs toward the ladies, taking whatever room that was left on the benches.

"Where y'all niggas at, shawty?" blasted Pooh sarcastically as the two approached.

"Boy, bye!" Laughed Malisha while the rest of the girls chuckled behind her.

"My baby, right here!" screamed Tawana, giving Pooh a big hug and juicy kiss. "Muah!" The flock of girls chuckled a little bit more.

Pooh blushed but nevertheless showed Tawana's friends he was affectionate, putting him out there like a casanova of some sort, embracing the stage play, ending it with a smack on her butt.

"You play too much, bae!" screamed Tawana. A little embarrassed now but turned on at the same time. She loved the roughness in Pooh, not so much of a choir boys but not too rugged. It was his demeanor that drew her to him.

The couple eventually settled down watching the game, enjoying the entertainment.

The Eagles was leading 27 to 17 against the Rams by time halftime was approaching. Harvey had two touchdowns, one off a sixty-seven-yard handoff and another off a twelve-yard screen pass play. He meant business, and Rizz watched like a proud father cheering on for his son, but instead, it was his little brother. Rizz seen potential in his little brother, a dream for him to make it to the big leagues and not fall victim to these streets. He kept Harvey away from the block. The only time he was allowed to come thru was if he had to run to the store or if he was going to the Boys & Girls club to workout. That was the only time you really would see Harvey around the way. He tried a couple times to sneak and hang out there, but Rizz found out somehow and would display a body beating to the public when he caught Harvey.

"Pow!" The gun goes off signaling that it was halftime. The players started running off the field towards their own sidelines. Fans started making their way toward the concession stands to get their refreshments and to lollygag. It looked like a pride's herd to a drinking hole in the jungle or outback sort to speak. Pooh could see John-John was already in line as he approached the stand but not really caring for him because he was looking for Black initially. Pooh brushed the notion off. Soon, a feeling swept the air like a bad vibe was forming. You know the one when you feel somebody watching you or have eyes on you, and you just can't fathom who or why and for what reason.

In the middle of Rizz and Pooh's conversation about Graph not making it to the game, they could spot John-John staring at them as if looks could kill. "You see dis lil nigga here!" boasts Rizz, pointing out the obvious to the rest of the fellas.

"Man, fuck dat nigga! We came to see a good game!" Pooh answered.

"You right. I ain't gon' start no shit! But dis nigga keep lookin' at me funny. Imma crack his shit!" added Rizz.

The boys order their food and proceed back to their seats, but to their surprise, they see John-John again still staring with blaze at them. Now surrounded by a few more of his fellas, Pooh could see that this little nigga had a reason for doing this. After so long of a staring contest, finally, Pooh spoke, "What, nigga!"

"Fuck you mean what nigga, you kno' what?" returned John-John. "What's up wit stealing my brotha car and robbing him? Huh, you bitch ass nigga!" he added.

"Fuck you talkin' 'bout, nigga. I ain't fuck wit your brotha shit nor car. What da fuck I need to steal a car for, nigga. I got my own, you clown! How da fuck you sound you fuckin' dummy!" blasted Pooh, "and my own bread, fuck you mean pussy!"

"Nigga, we kno" it was y'all WP niggas. Don't think we don't kno' about Graph in 1442, nigga! My people seen 'em in and outta dere!" spurts John-John. "You think we dumb or somethin nigga!" he added.

Throughout all the hype and yelling that was going on, Pooh caught what John-John said about Graph being in their area. He started thinking to himself like, *No dis nigga didn't do dat shit! Fuck!* But nevertheless, if it went down, he had his cousin back no doubt for whatever the reason. Rizz and the rest of the posse was waiting and itching like they could careless. They knew the deal.

"I don't care if you blind bitch. Dat shit don't have nuttin to do wit me, nigga!" Pooh blasts. "Do somethin' if you feel otherwise, pussy!" he finisheed.

The words triggered John-John making him angry to where he threw his soda bottle he was holding at Pooh, but anticipating the move, Pooh dodged the bottle countering with a right hook to John-John's jaw staggering him back. Pooh connected another two-piece combo dropping John-John flat on his back. He mounted on top of John-John, but before he could let off another punch, one of John-John's boys blindsided him off top, sending Pooh rolling. That moment right there rang the alarm for the rest of the brigade, with Rizz leading the way like a rhino ready to pummel something.

Chaos started, and no one was really safe. Fights spawned then started to spread like a wildfire throughout the oval shaped bowl field. Whether you wanted to fight or not, you had no choice because the game turned into a gladiator ring. Debris started flying, and the sounds of profanity shouting plus kids crying masked the atmosphere. How did something so sacred go horribly wrong? All it takes is a small spark, nothing more nothing less. The cops was outnumbered, so they were outweighed for the moment 'til backup arrived, trying to control what they possibly could for the time being. Soon after, the squad's cars arrived, most of the mayhem dispersed in different directions.

"Imma see you, you bitch ass, nigga!" screamed John-John, as one of his boys was dragging him off. Pointing at Pooh in a threatening manner like his fingers could shoot bullets while bleeding from the face.

"Fuck you, pussy. I'm outchea erryday!" Pooh replied. "My heart don't pump no kool-aid, nigga!"

Rizz taps Pooh alerting him that it was time to go since the police had arrived. Also the fact that his forearm was bleeding because one of them Island boys sliced him when he was pounding him out. Couldn't take him to the county hospital, they would ask questions that needed no answers, so they thought it was best he hit the city hospital instead.

"We out, yo!" screamed Pooh getting whoever's attention that was with him out there. Rizz had his arm wrapped in his T-shirt, keeping the pressure on the cut so he didn't lose too much blood. The scene went from 0 to 60 instantly without a blink of the eye.

"You good, my nigga?" Jay asked Rizz.

"Yea, ain't shit but a scratch!" Rizz answered. "Dem niggas kno' what time it is!"

"Yo, I kno' where dey gon' be later. Shawty hit me wit dat info," Jay whispered. "But now you banged up!" he added, not trying to let no one else hear him.

"Fuck allat, I'm gravy! Imma link you wit Malik and catch up after I get cleaned up! Aight?" Rizz finished.

"Aight, big bro, we gon' stake it out. They at the Super 8 but don't kno' which room yet, but hit me when you ready," ended Jay.

"Bet!" screamed Rizz as he hops in the car with Pooh ready to be taken to the city hospital, which was a longer ride down the highway.

By the time Pooh and Rizz reached the exit to the highway, his cellphone goes off. "Yo!" he answered.

"What's da deal, bro, 'bout to board dis flight," the voice said, now realizing it was Graph calling. "Told you I'll hit you before I leave, nigga. Wat you forgot?" Graph continued.

"Nah, bro, I didn't. Shit jus' jumped off at the game between us and them Island niggas, bro! I mean, wild crazy, the boys had to come shut shit down, so we broke out!" Pooh rambled. "Not to mention Rizz got stabbed, psst. I'm takin' 'em to da spiddal as we speak!"

"Hold up what you mean, is bro good?" Graph asked. The elevation of concern rising in his voice. "Who and how tho?"

Graph was asking so many questions back to back that Pooh couldn't keep up with answering them all.

"Bro, good for da moment, how 'bout you tho? Errythin, set, we back on track?" Pooh asked. "What's da movement?"

"Yea, errythin set. I'm tryna see what's da deal wit y'all niggas and all dis bullshit happens psst!" answered Graph.

"Look, bro, don't worry 'bout dis end here. We got it! Jus' handle dat pipeline wit SC so we back on!" blasted Pooh.

Graph sat in silence for a second, not because of Pooh's response but because he felt relief that he didn't have to be there to know his niggas handled business when it came to rumbling with them Island niggas.

"Oh, but I do got a bone to pick wit you when you get back, fam!" added Pooh.

"What's dat?" blasted Graph.

"Don't worry, jus' hit me when you touchdown, and get settled in da room, Aight? Augusta, right, dat's where you headed?" Pooh spitted.

"Yea, I'll be there no later than eleven. I'll hit you around midnight," Graph returned.

"Y'all niggas jus be safe 'til I get back!"

"You do da same, big bro, be safe out dere? Handle dat and come on home, nuttin else!" ended Pooh.

"Cool, you already!" ended Graph. The phones go dead and Pooh focuses back on getting Rizz to the hospital.

"What dat nigga was talkin' 'bout?" went Rizz.

"Ain't shit, he 'bouta head OT tonight so we should be back up and running soon. He said he'll be in Augusta by eleven or so," replied Pooh.

Rizz had a memory come to his mind once he heard Augusta. He remembered his dad along with Graph's dad Lenny and a few of his other fellas use to move in and out of Georgia, particularly the Augusta region. They use to run cigarettes and liquor amongst other things before the crack game blew up, back and forth up to the hood making a hustle. Rizz couldn't really remember too much details about their old head's ring, just that they were familiar with that area. Maybe they were related or connected in some way down there. It wasn't no telling. Come to think of it, Kato always bragged about his brother use to run shit before he took over, but he never mentioned the name Southern Comfort just SC. That's when a light hits Rizz once he puts the initials together.

Could it be da same nigga? Rizz thought to himself. The puzzle was coming together but slowly. Rizz turns to Pooh and asks, "Yo, remember back in da day, da nigga Kato use to brag about his older brother SC? Supposedly da nigga dat fuck wit Graph's mom before he was born! Started beefin wit Lenny and my pops. No one knows what happened to 'em after Lenny got killed, and my dad got locked up!"

"Vaguely, why?" answered Pooh.

"You don't think that's the same nigga dat we been grabbin from, do you?" replied Rizz.

A shocking look comes to Pooh's face as he's pulling into the emergency room parking lot area. A look of horror drapes his face for he started to shiver, knowing if this was true then Graph could be in trouble not knowing that Southern Comfort could have had something to do with his dad's Lenny's death. No one but the ones at that time knew the full story or the truth to what happened to Lenny, but the younger generation caught bits and pieces of it. That was another reason why the streets thought Graph took out Kato because he was related to SC, for the revenge. Either way, all bad and could be a trap setup. Pooh started to panic trying to call Graph's cell, but it went to voice mail. He dials again and gets the same response.

"Shit!" he screamed.

Rizz could tell by the way Pooh was moving that he had struck a nerve of some sort. Graph's phone was still going to the voice mail.

"I don't kno', bro, but if it is, we gotta warn dat nigga befo it's too late!" Pooh answered finally getting his thoughts back. "But dis nigga phone goin' to da voice mail. I think he already on da plane, fuck!"

"Damn, son. Yea, now to think of it didn't Luck say dey got hit in a Buick for da drop?" Rizz asked.

"Yea, why?" replied Pooh.

"And didn't dat bitch ass nigga John-John say Black car got stolen?" Rizz continued.

"Yea, why what's your point, nigga?" spitted Pooh. "I'm sayin, think about it, someone put us in the mix wit dem Island niggas on one end right? Then da work comes in fucked up on da last go round, shit don't seem odd to you, my nigga?" asked Rizz.

"Now dat you mention it, shit is a big coinkidink! But why now after all these years, bro? A ten-year grudge?" returned Pooh. "Niggas didn't prove shit on either end, so what's da point!"

"Rumor has it, dat my pops and Lenny lifted three mill off some cat down south but never knew who da person was," added Rizz.

Tension brewed in the air from the two as they were taking a trip down memory lane trying to piece together the then and now. This would be bad, bad all the way around if something was to happen to Graph especially with no backup and no way to warn him. A part of guilt swept the two also knowing they shouldn't let Graph take the trip alone, but the spur of the moment kept them from going which happened to be Southern Comfort's doing.

"I heard dat befo but never knew if it was true, my nigga!" returned Pooh. "Imma try and get ahold of dis nigga, and make him abort 'til we figure dis shit out fully! Lemme kno' what da doc says when you get out of dere, Aight?" ended Pooh.

"Bet, I'll be good. Imma have Linda come scoop me. She lives right up da road a few blocks! I'll hit you when I get back around da way!" finished Rizz, while getting out of the car and walking into the emergency room sliding doors looking for a doctor not minding the desk clerk speaking to him.

"Hello! … Sir! … Sir! … You jus' can't go back dere, sir!"

CHAPTER 19

Mayhem and Murder, M&Ms

Everybody was waiting on the word of Rizz's well-being, plus the fact that Pooh couldn't get ahold of Graph. Two problems at once was stirring around as the rest of the crew tried to settle down from the earlier conflictions. Manny and Luck had two house parties planned for the festivities after the homecoming game. The word got passed throughout the city for the people to come enjoy themselves and celebrate the city win. From bottles to chicks and more was the highlight for the night. Sky's the limit and wasn't no telling where you were going to end up at later.

Pooh called to check to make sure Tawana had made it home safely after the melee. The conversation between the two was short because her mother was around at the time so she couldn't talk, but she told him that they needed to talk because it was important. So after he checked in with his girl, he then made a call to Luck.

"Ring!"

"Yo, what's goodie!" answered Luck.

"What's da move?" Pooh asked.

"Shit, we got da parties lined up tonight. What you tryna do, bruh?" returned Luck. "You comin thru?"

"Nah, prolly not got some shit I gotta handle!" Pooh answered.

Being discreet with what was on his mind, he didn't portray any hints toward Luck and kept him out the loop. He felt to keep the info to himself hoping that the whole plug thing was a hoax and he didn't blow shit out of proportion. Pooh last move was to spark a riot if there was no need to. Graph was all alone, and no one was around to watch his back and that was what was eating Pooh.

"Aight, fam. Well if you come out, you kno' where we at, out in da SMU!" ended Luck. "Cool!"

After an hour or so, Rizz pops up on the block with his arm bandaged up propped in a sling. The fellas could see he was upset about the situation so they stayed out his way and fed him blunts and shots of Bacardi to calm him down. Before long, the block was lit up with all the various characters that inhabited it. The meeting grounds for the jungle recipients to roam around freely.

Rizz was waiting on word from Jay and Malik. So to burn time, he hung out with Luck out in Da Greens getting a buzz until he heard otherwise. His initial plan was still set up, to get revenge on the Island niggas at the Super 8 motel and dish out a little payback. The streets was in a standstill, with not good much product floating around. Since the coke was cut on the last go, it was more of a burden to get rid of. When folks start complaining on the quality of your work in anything you do, then it becomes a bad rap on your name, even your city. That's something they wanted to be known for, especially controlling the drug money. Pooh was in serious thoughts, so he meditated to himself, keeping his mind at ease and hoping for the better. Steering clear of the fellas so he could plot his next move to compensate for all the fucked-up circumstances that was going on. He just wanted to be alone to think and calculate. Waiting on the call from Graph made him even more weary and anxious, hoping he would hear from him soon and know his cousin in crime was safe. It's 10:59 p.m. The clock was ticking slow as a slug for Pooh as he watched the second hand rotate around the circle facing. He knew that the rest of the fellas were going to enjoy themselves, but he just wasn't in a partying mood.

Finally, Rizz got the call he was waiting for while hanging with Luck and Manny. The two could see that Rizz had a different agenda for the night by the way he kept looking out the window as if he was waiting for someone or something. After a few minutes, you could hear a honk outside of the house.

"Beep! Yo, I'm out fellas. I'll catch up wit y'all later, fam!" Luck and Manny walked with him to the car that was waiting for him, seeing that it was Jay and Malik inside it.

"Yo, y'all sure y'all don't wanna chill? We got some more bitches coming thru, bro!" spitted Manny.

"Not right now, maybe after we handle dis bizness!" went Rizz. "Got some shit to take care of!"

You could tell the trio were anxious to leave and handle whatever it was they needed to handle, not giving room for extracurricular activities.

"If it don't get too late, we'll swing back thru and bring summin!" added Rizz, while hopping in the car.

"Aight bet, bruh, y'all be safe!" ended Luck.

The car pulls off while leaving Manny and Luck looking in amazement, like what were these niggas up to. *Maybe goin' to a strip-club,* the two thought, but who knows when the two were together; and now that Malik was hanging with them could mean just about anything. "Fuck it!" they said as they went back inside the house to party, not giving a second thought to what Rizz and the gang had up their sleeves.

So on the ride to the hotel where the sting operation was going down at, Jay spoke, "Yo, I found out da room. It's number 133 at da supa 8, dem niggas in there right now! I got errythin right here!" he spitted as he's showing Rizz all the hardware and black attire he had for him.

"Bet, pass me dat shit!" blurted Rizz ecstatically.

Malik was already suited and booted for the caper at hand, still exposing his face because he didn't put on his ski mask yet still waiting 'til they reached the hotel. Rizz was sorely getting himself together still tender from his previous wounds, trying to get stuff in perspective. He was suiting up slowly but surely. The car soon came to a screeching halt when it entered the hotel parking lot, dropping off the two by the back entrance leaving a space for a perfect undetectable getaway. After Rizz and Jay hopped out the car, they posted by the back door pulling their masks down and cocking their guns. They could spot where Malik had parked so they could pinpoint how long it was going to take them to flee from the building to the car and from the car to the other side of the city. Also they knew that the room the Island niggas were in closer to the back entrance on the bottom floor, an easy way to get in and out without any problems. It was now or never, and the two knew it was that time to make shit happen; so they lined up at the door and took a deep breath before they went to kick it in.

They could hear whoever from the outside and could smell the weed smoke that circulated and staggered the hallway. It definitely second the motion that this was the room they were looking for.

"On da count of three! One! Two! Three!

"Boom!"

The door comes off the hinge instantly creating a hole when Rizz kicked it, exposing the inside and what was in it. More smoke came out the room as they bum rushed in groping up everyone they could see.

"Get da fuck down, down! Don't nobody move shit!" they screamed, getting the attention of the people in the hotel party. Both were waving and flashing matching twin 40 caliber handguns using them for crowd control. Soon as they had the room under control, they spotted Black and his little brother in the corner hiding behind some chicks.

"Bring your bitch ass ova here!" Rizz screamed to them. Jay made his way towards them to yank them up but couldn't see their hands that were hiding behind the girls. As soon as Jay got closer to them, you heard a shot and a scream. Black had his gun out the whole time to where they couldn't see it so he attempted some action movie type shit by trying to shoot thru one of the girls that was standing in front of him, hoping to strike Jay as he got closer. It didn't work out as he had planned it to because now Jay let off his handgun in that section, firing at will. He catches his little brother John-John in the chest from the blaze he unleashed, sending him rolling back towards the coffee table. Black starts shooting back now frantically "Pow, POW, POW!" returning back fire inside the small quarters. Jay didn't have a chance to swing and line up with Black and shoot by the time he returned fire. The bullets struck Jay in the chest, pushing him into the wall like he was being tackled. Rizz was on point but too late to save his comrade but avenged him by striking Black down. Rizz could see he had the drop on Black once he hit him, so he walked up and finished off the job by shooting Black in the head twice. "Pop, Pop!"

Through all the melee that was going on with the bitches screaming and everyone dispersing, Rizz could only think about his young boy who had just got murdered in front of him. But with Jay still breathing faintly, he scooped him up and rushed him out the room through the back door to the car. Malik was sitting in the car waiting for the two to come out, when he spotted Rizz carrying Jay, that's when he swung the car up to get them.

"What da fuck happened?" Malik screamed as Rizz threw Jay in the backseat.

"Yo, don't worry jus drive, bro! We gotta get dis nigga to a hospital ASAP!" Rizz blasted.

The blood was coming from Jay's chest plate making a puddle in the back of the car. His breathing was getting more shallow by the minute, so Rizz told Malik to hurry and take the bridge. Once they made it to the bridge that's when Rizz rolls down the window and throws the two handguns out into the river. They were moving in top speed, flying down the highway until a patrol car clocked their speed. The squad car threw its lights on trying to pull them over, but that didn't stop them so it became a high speed chase.

"Ah, shit!" they screamed as the flashing lights were burrowing in on them, but that didn't slow them down at all, not one bit; but actually making Malik speed up even faster now trying to lose them. But it was impossible to lose the police once they had alerted back up. The police managed to put down a spike strip in the direction they were headed, ripping the tires straight off the rims. Malik lost control of the car sending them crashing into a guardrail. "CRAKK!" The metal intertwined together like it was magnetic. Malik was still conscious and mobile enough to hop out the car and flee into the woods on foot. The cops didn't pursue the chase with him on foot because they had the crashed vehicle to worry about. On the other hand, Rizz was in the car still unconscious, bleeding from the head and Jay was in the backseat dead now from the extra injuries. When the police did their investigation and prowling of the scene that's when they discovered the two in the car, they looked in bewilderment. *What da fuck!* they thought. *They done stumbled into some shit tonight!*

Word traveled around town later that night about the shootout at the Super 8, but no one knew who was behind the hit. Some people had a clue to it but no concrete evidence was established yet.

The house party was going crazy until it got interrupted by a phone call from a chick who heard the news. Manny and Luck sat in silence looking at each other once they were relayed the news in awe and disbelief.

"No, it can't be!" The looks on their faces were saying this, hoping that it wasn't them and somebody else, but another phone call solidified it, that Rizz had crashed. The police was guarding his room, waiting to lock him up after he got cleared, and Jay died on the way to the hospital. This was a bad blow to the city nation, and so now the party that once was for celebrating the Eagles win, was now turned into a grieving session for the loss. A double tragedy, when you lose one to the grave and another to the cage. Crazy how life can switch up on you in an instance, giving you no room for improvement but error, sickening and unimaginable all in the same sense. Even though it was fall season, the night air was hot due to the friction that was going on. Everybody was acting frantic, trying to find out the background of the situation that caused the city to uproar. What madness? You would thought the Pope himself died out there the way folks were running away with the story, 12:27 a.m.

Pooh had no recollection to anything that was going since he was in solitary mode as far as to Rizz's side plan that went astray, and Jay's untimely demise. All he was concentrating on was the phone call from Graph.

The phone rings at 12:30 on the dot when Graph finally called, Pooh answers it quickly.

"Yo, my nigga I think Southern Comfort is indeed SC, bruh!"

"The one that had beef wit your pops Lenny back in da day!" Pooh rambled, not giving Graph a chance to speak.

"Who!" blurted Graph. Not conjuring up the memories quite so quick.

"Da nigga Kato brother supposedly! You kno' who I'm talkin about, nigga!" continued Pooh.

"Vaguely, but dat nigga is dead, bro, from what I heard! He got murdered in dat robbery so I was told! And what da fuck dat got to do wit me?" returned Graph. He had just finished checking into his hotel where he was set up to stay at, walking through the halls while talking on his phone with Pooh. Once he located his room, he inserts the key turning the knob to enter all in the same motion while conversing with Pooh still on the phone. He wanted to wait 'til he got inside the room to further discuss the dead coming back to life. As Graph opens the door and walks in to turn the lights on so he could put his luggage down and get settled, that's when he observed Southern Comfort in the chair smoking a cigar as he normally would, when the lights came on. His heart jumps because he was caught off guard, not thinking no one was going to be there unexpectedly. Pooh could hear on the other end of the phone how Graph yelped a little bit.

"Yo!" he screamed.

Graph didn't respond, still getting accustomed to the fact of Southern Comfort's unannounced entry.

"Yo!" again went Pooh.

Graph sets his stuff down in the room and speaks "What's up, Boss!" That's when Pooh realized that Graph was in the presence of Southern Comfort, and it was a set up.

"YOO! GET DA FUCK OUTTA DERE, YO!" blasted Pooh. Trying to hypnotize or regain control to Graph's trance, but by the time he realized what Pooh was saying, it was too late to turn back out the room because Southern Comfort's mysterious associate popped out the bathroom to block the door when Graph made a step backwards. He snatches the phone from Graph throwing it to the ground shattering it, cutting off the connection with Pooh.

Pooh looks at his phone in shock trying not to think the worst. He dials again. Graph's phone went straight to voice mail. He dials again, and the same thing happens. He was numb because at this

point there was nothing he could do; but if something was to happen, he was going to be the first to react. It was a must, and now his
family was on the line.

Pooh tried to call everybody he could think of but no one
answered because of unavailability. He would have to pop up on Luck
because Luck was hosting the house parties. Rizz was handcuffed to a
hospital bed incapacitated, and to top it off, Jay's body was heading
to the morgue now. Life as itself was unravelling for Pooh as he tried
to pull himself together for he didn't cry. He stayed head strong in
the matter and said to himself "We gon' handle dis shit, one way or
da other! Fo you, GRAPH!"

Graph looked at Southern Comfort in confusion and frustration and then spoke, "What's dis about, my nigga?"

"I like you, youngin'. I really do, but it's deeper den dat!"
answered SC. "You see dis scar rite here?" he pointed at while saying
this, "You can thank your mother and father for dis!"

ABOUT THE AUTHOR

Karl Rodgers, better known as Karl "Buck" Rodgers, was born in Killeen, Texas, on April 7, 1981. The only surviving son of his mother, who was a soldier for the US military, both left the south side of Chicago to start the journey of his life back in the mid '80s. Touching over twenty states and a country under his belt, Germany to add, made his imagination and creativity to grow and blossom into expressive shapes and forms. Eventually settling down in Aberdeen, MD just north of Baltimore, made this his home for the years to come. At one point and time in his childhood, Karl wanted to be an artist painting and drawing, but soon found out that his mind was indeed a paintbrush within its own. A passionate and descriptive writer by day, but a mild-mannered father who loves his kids and family that works on an everyday living just like the next man by night.

CPSIA information can be obtained
at www.ICGtesting.com
Printed in the USA
LVHW091703290420
654637LV00007B/647